MW00380808

To: Cabinets To Go
Blaine —

# RATTLED

First hardcover edition December 2021

Library of Congress Control Number: 2021920498

Hardcover ISBN: 978-0-578-97246-6
eBook ISBN: 978-0-578-97247-3

Book Design by www.BookDesigners.com

For information about special discounts
for bulk purchases, please contact:
AllisonDalvit@Gmail.com

Ross Shafer Consultants, Inc.
10589 Dacre Place
Lone Tree, CO 80124

www.RossShafer.com

Photograph Credits appear on page 190

# RATTLED

## Crazy A** Stories *of* Extreme Resilience *to* Help You Go *from* Shook *to*...Solid

Ross Shafer    Allison Dalvit

*with* Cass Jacoby

# DISCLAIMER

The stories you will read in this book actually happened to us and might possibly happen to you someday. We have tried to recreate the events, locales, and conversations from our memories. But you know how memories, trauma, and wine can affect such. That said, to protect privacy, in some instances we have changed the names and occupations of individuals. We also cannot control how you interpret the stories in this book. Therefore, the authors do not assume and hereby disclaim any liability to any of you for any loss, damage, or disruption caused by errors or omissions, whether such errors or omissions result from negligence, accident, or any other cause. Fortunately for you, we do not dispense advice on weight or hair loss, your future health, or how to get richer than your neighbors. As long as you agree, you will most likely enjoy reading how we got here.

# INTRODUCTION

# Been Rattled Lately?

*Of course, you have!*

No matter how well you have planned for life's unplanned contingencies, your life will be upended by an unexpected event or a terrifying consequence you didn't see coming. Like what? Like falling in love with the exact wrong person for you. Like having your career derailed because a coworker started an untrue rumor you couldn't defend. Like the financial investment you thought was bulletproof...yet wiped out your savings overnight. How about a global pandemic that forced you to lock down and mask up? There are thousands of other blindsiding U-turns waiting to rattle your future in gut-wrenching new ways.

All of that (and much more) has happened to us, too. No matter how confident we thought we were, unforeseen circumstances have left us sideswiped, surprised, and crushed about what to do next.

So, in this book, you will find 30 of our most bizarre life experiences—and how we went from being totally shaken...to getting back on solid ground, again.

We also think you will be entertained.

As network TV talk and game show hosts, entertainers, television producers, business owners, and real estate investors, we constantly found ourselves out of control trying to make a living— dependent upon the vagaries of pop culture, ever-changing news cycles, boneheaded coworkers, and getting caught up in fleeting fame. As we told these stories to friends, we made them cry, laugh, cringe, and ultimately enjoy the rescue efforts we concocted to solve our predicaments.

The result is an unvarnished account of the good and bad decisions we made, the bad advice we took, how we collapsed and how we rallied past our missteps to be healthy, happy, and safe.

*—Ross Shafer*      *—Allison Dalvit*
*...with Cass Jacoby*

# WHEN YOU FIND YOURSELF RATTLED...

# CHAPTER 1

# Be Brief

*By Ross Shafer*

## Why Read This Story?

*We all get frustrated with people who talk too much and end up saying nothing. Maybe that's what you do? If you want to get more done with less words, this story is for you.*

One minute I was the King of the world.

The next minute I was dreadfully humbled by Microsoft founder Bill Gates.

In 1984, I was hosting a comedy/talk TV show in Seattle, Washington, titled *Almost Live!*

We could snag big name guests like Jerry Seinfeld, Joe Walsh (the Eagles), and Ellen DeGeneres. But we could never land the world's richest man, Microsoft founder Bill Gates. (He lived nearby.)

We asked him often, but he always refused.

I dare say, he could benefit from being on our show. Our audience was young and we had just launched a national campaign to change the Washington state song to *Louie, Louie.*

We were hot. Surely, Bill Gates knew who I was.

Getting to him was still difficult.

As the relentless man that I am, I finally tracked down somebody who knew a guy, who knew a woman, who was acquainted with another woman, who was Bill's personal assistant. Even better, this woman was a fan of our TV show and talked me up to Bill.

I sent her T-shirts, coffee mugs, DVDs, and one day she called to say she had set up a meeting with myself and William Henry Gates III.

I knew Bill liked cable knit sweaters so I wore one I thought he'd admire. (Pardon me, that just sounded like I was dealing with pre-date jitters.)

I got to the Microsoft campus early, met the assistant, and she invited me to visit their well-appointed, private employee commissary. All of the food and drinks were free. I had a thick grilled cheese and turkey sandwich. As I sat down, I was immediately recognized by a group of maybe 20 employees. I signed some autographs and took some pictures.

What a welcome! This was going to be a cake walk!

An assistant (to Bill's assistant) collected me from the commissary saying, "Bill is ready for you."

The jitters returned.

Nervousness was new to me. I don't get starstruck. I've met a cavalcade of "stars" and I've performed for 20,000 people in stadiums.

All I was there to do was meet Bill, make him laugh, gin up a little rapport, and invite him to do a six-minute guest spot on my fashionable talk show.

I made my way to the outside foyer of his office and his

personal assistant grinned, "Go on in."

My back straight and my smile gleaming, I dashed over the door's threshold to see him.

At 5' 10" tall and thin, Bill Gates looked smaller than I expected.

I was casual and ready to wing this. (I know celebs don't like to be treated special.)

I said, "Hello, Bill."

He didn't look up. "Ross?" he said as he was staring down at what looked like a nine-inch thick dossier on world domination.

He finally lifted his eyes to mine and said, "Be brief."

Be brief? No pleasantries? People who change the world are apparently in a big hurry.

I think I laughed a little, but he was not amused. He was telling me, don't dawdle, sonny.

I felt like a kid who had been scolded.

I was mentally editing what I should say next, cutting and pasting intentions in my head. I was literally unable to organize thoughts. Nothing was coming out and he was looking at me like, "Somebody gave YOU a TV show?" I finally spit out a couple of broken phrases, in no intelligible order.

Bill short-circuited my bumbling with, "Thanks for comin' in," and he slipped through a side door.

Bill Gates was never a guest on my show.

"Be brief" was a Bill Gates test and I blew it.

And, you know what? I should have beat him at that game. I got my start in show business as a stand-up comedian. I succeeded as a stand-up by editing every joke down to its five-second essence. More laughs per minute. In his 1602 play *Hamlet*,

Shakespeare coined the phrase, "Brevity is the soul of wit." And for the ensuing 400 years, everyone knows we are at our most interesting when we are BRIEF.

I have never been as disorganized since.

We should all have a policy of BEING BRIEF. Being brief is getting to the point when you are talking to your boss. Being brief is cutting to the chase when you're telling a story at a party. Being brief is listening to other people talk and not trying to out-verbalize them.

My mistake was trying to impress Bill Gates with who I was (a clown who wings it)…instead of preparing to understand who he was (a man who is vigorously prepared).

## What's In This For You?

*You will get more respect in life if you learn to Be Brief when explaining what you want. Be brief when you write an email. Be brief when you are defending your point of view. Be Brief when telling a story to your friends and family—unless, on the off chance, they ask to hear more.*

# CHAPTER 2

# Trust Yourself

*By Allison Dalvit*

## Why Read This Story?

*You have probably been faced with dozens of gut-wrenching decisions in your life. You got advice from friends, family, and experts. Did you ever wish you had the courage to ignore everyone and trust your gut? If so, this story is for you.*

"Your baby is dying."

My OBGYN's verdict crushed me. No one prepares you for a failing pregnancy. For 20 weeks, my life was all about belly touches and choosing baby names (we picked Mikaela). Suddenly my doctor is lobbying to abort.

"What does that mean?"

The doctor ignored me, "It's too soon to tell why your child isn't growing. We suggest an abortion while you can still get one."

I was barely able to conceive. My last pregnancy took three years to arrive—with a fertility drug. I burned through countless boxes of pregnancy tests and each time I got my period, I sobbed in the shower, knowing I wouldn't be a mother.

The doctor was droning on while my mind reached its only conclusion: Losing my child is not an option.

"I won't abort."

The doctor was finally listening.

"Okay then," he said, "We believe her amniotic fluid has a virus, meaning your daughter will be born very ill or with Down syndrome." None of this mattered, I wanted my baby.

The doctor hedged, "Our best outcome for your child is rare. We would be hoping the umbilical cord has not developed. An undeveloped umbilical cord was rare but meant she was very sick. Your daughter will be born with complications."

Now, I was the one doing the ignoring.

*"If you tell me what I can do, I will end this year with a baby girl in my arms."* The doctor tested my resolve with, "If you insist on keeping her, you will need full bed rest. Eat non-stop. If you aren't eating, you should be drinking Gatorade. You'll need to see me every day to get ultrasounds."

This was the glimmer I needed to save my baby.

I followed the doctor's orders with the rigor of a Special Ops Lieutenant. My doctors injected me with hormones that covered my body in rashes. I consumed more Gatorade in one day than the entire NBA did in a season. I would not fall asleep at my post. Not for a second of the next five months. I was driven by the vision of seeing that baby girl smiling back at me.

I'd soon learn the news wasn't getting any better.

In the 28th week (of a typical 40-week pregnancy), my daily ultrasound showed Mikaela was still losing weight. I was whisked to the hospital to get amniotic fluid extracted for testing. The procedure required I remain dead-still as, what looked like, a foot-long needle was inserted into my abdomen. Any involuntary twitch could misdirect the needle into the fetus. Staring at the ultrasound, I watched the needle swim within millimeters of Mikaela's head.

Within seconds, the amniocentesis revealed another 5-alarm emergency.

The medical team immediately wheeled me to the birth ward for a C-section. I didn't expect to be laying on an ice-cold metal slab, flanked by a team of doctors. Frightening metal tools were everywhere. An anesthesiologist numbed the lower part of my body. After enough time, the surgeon used a kind of laser knife against my stomach. Giant plumes of smoke from my burning flesh filled the room with a stench that disgusted my nostrils. Think burning hair and roasted roadkill. My eyes darted across the room to find my mom on the other side of the body tent. Her eyes bulged, reacting to the sight of my bladder being gently removed and placed beside me on a metal tray.

It wasn't until this moment that doubt crept in. Had I made the right choice? Did my iron will make this worse? Did my unbridled optimism under-prepare me for failure? All I could do was surrender. I'd done my best. I tried.

Completely spent, I saw the doctors hold up something impossibly small. Mikaela was here in some form. Her features were un-carved. Her eyes and ears were smoothed over by a translucent layer of skin. Was she alive? Must be because the nurses rushed her into another room to start tests and incubation. In the rarest of miracles, my baby had survived a three-month premature birth and the disconnect of an umbilical cord.

Weak as I was, I needed to see my baby. My doctors knew better than to argue. They slumped me in a wheelchair and pushed me to my daughter's incubator. I recall whispering to my little girl, "We did it, we beat the odds to meet each other."

Mikaela was kept in an ICU 24-hour care incubator to finish growing. I never left her side. As much as I wanted to bring Kaela home, we weren't out of the woods. At her two-pound featherweight (down from three pounds), she could easily forget to breathe while feeding. To take her home I would need to take an overnight test to prove I could resuscitate her if she stopped breathing. That night at the ICU was spent with Mikaela on my chest. I don't know if I could rescue a baby with CPR today, but I certainly did that night. Throughout our stay, she stopped breathing a few times and I passed the test. Mikaela could finally come home.

Mikaela slowly became a perfectly normal, healthy, strong baby. Herculean, I'd say. She could lean against my hip and wrap her fingers around my arm, clinging to me like a monkey. Despite the terrifying possibility of her being physically or mentally challenged as a child, our fears never materialized. She went on to be a superior athlete and captain of her high school cheerleading team. Mikaela also graduated from the University of Colorado, Boulder, with a degree in neuroscience. Today, she works in the healthcare field and it would not surprise me if she invented a medicine or medical procedure that would help heal the world.

Every day, I am grateful that I listened to my intuition and fought for my daughter's life. The planet is better with Mikaela in it.

## What's In This For You?

*Conventional wisdom says we should trust the experts. Experts can give you the facts of their experience—but when all of the experts go home, you are the person left to live with the consequences. Your own will and discipline are inexplicable factors no expert can evaluate.*

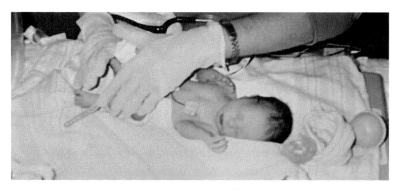

*My 2-pound preemie, Mikaela Marie.*

*Mikaela earned a Bachelor's degree in Neuroscience from CU Boulder and now works in the medical field.*

# CHAPTER 3

# Stay Home

*By Ross Shafer*

### Why Read This Story?

*A promotion that requires you to move to a different city, state or even a different country should not be decided lightly. I hope this story makes you dig deep within your heart before you say, "Let's start over somewhere else."*

Up until I was five years old, I loved my life.

As far as I knew, my dad was a popular car salesman in McMinnville, Oregon, who would throw fun parties at our home. Everyone laughed when my father dislodged his dentures, put on funny hats, and pantomimed the words to his favorite 78 rpm records. Always a lot of laughter in our home.

Yet in a flash, the idyllic life my brother Clell and I loved was disrupted.

A gigantic yellow Mayflower moving truck arrived one morning.

My mother hustled us out of bed to tell us we were leaving our home, moving 35 miles away to the big city of Portland.

Strangers wrapping my bed in cellophane. Hairy men carrying our fridge outside. Are we going to an orphanage?

I had no clue that Dad hated his car salesman job. For months, he had been taking night classes to become "a tire and battery rep" with the Richfield Oil Company (which later morphed into ARCO).

When Dad "graduated" from his course of study, he was offered a great job. Literally overnight, he had to buy a suit and follow the money. (Think Mad Men.)

By that next Monday, Mayflower dropped us off at a dingy hovel (our new home). Without streetlights, everything outside looked dangerous. While my little brother slept in my parent's room, I was relegated to the scary, spider-infested basement. A couple months later, my baby brother Scott arrived.

I didn't even know how to meet other kids. I felt scared and unwelcome.

First and second grade came and went slowly. I took accordion lessons against my will.

During the summer before third grade, Dad landed a surprise promotion that demanded we move to Medford, Oregon, 300 miles away.

The Mayflower truck was back.

My third school year was rough. Kids teased me that my head looked square. A bully left a dead bull snake on my bike. In fourth grade I made two good friends—T.J. Morris (an expert water skier) and Bill Singler (a great football player). I haven't spoken to either of them since.

During the summer we relocated again.

I started the fifth grade 150 miles away, in rainy Salem, Oregon.

This time, as an 11-year-old, I didn't even try to make friends. I was angry enough to fake self-confidence. I told kids, "We move a lot. I've lived in three different cities." I was surprised that made me popular. A world traveler? For once, I felt kinda special.

In sixth grade, I met my first girlfriend, Cindy Southwick. Before Cindy, I never thought of girls as pretty. I wrangled a job cleaning the horse barn where she kept her pony. One afternoon, she kissed me in her tree house. I floated home.

The next day, you can imagine how heartbroken I was to see a fourth Mayflower truck in our driveway.

Cindy and I promised to write to each other every week.

I kept that promise. I never heard from her again.

I didn't give a rat's ass that my father got another raise. Resentment raged in me for how he kept torching my world! Without consideration, he plopped our family down 350 miles away in Federal Way, Washington. Boeing Aircraft country.

As a seventh grader, I vowed never to move with my parents again. If I ever saw another Mayflower truck at my house, I would join a carnival.

Years passed. I finally settled into a familiar life with my friends, a love affair with cars, sports, and good summer jobs that paid for gas and milkshakes.

I graduated from high school as a first team all-conference linebacker and looked forward to my college football scholarship.

After my freshman year, I came home to my dad crowing that he'd won his biggest promotion ever. It meant uprooting from

Washington state to homestead in Walnut Creek, California…
800 miles away.

I couldn't locate a nearby carnival, so instead, I proposed to
my high school girlfriend, and we got married.

I realize how detached that sounds. I was barely 20 and,
without recognizing it, my brain had become numb and selfish.
I would create what my parents couldn't—stability.

After college, as a young husband, I took a couple of decent
paying jobs, had two wonderful sons, owned homes; yet I was
feeling the same frustrations my father must have felt years
ago— wanting to provide a better life for us.

I quit my best job because I was obsessed with becoming a
stand-up comedian.

Why comedy? One night, I went to a comedy club and saw
that comedians were showered with the human acceptance I had
missed as a nomadic child. I concocted a fast-track formula for
success and (within two years) I won a major comedy competition, which propelled me into the big leagues.

The more successful I became the more out-of-town travel
was required. But since I saw my father pull this off, I equated
success with travel.

I was supporting my family (all four of us) yet gone from home
60 percent of the time. There were no cell phones or FaceTime. I
called from phone booths in hotel lobbies.

The constant travel and transient nature of smokey night
club work wore down my marriage.

My young wife couldn't see how hard I worked to provide a
better life for my family.

I couldn't see how hard she was trying to create stability, safety, and security.

When I got divorced from their mother, my little boys were only three and five.

With little remorse, I moved from Washington state to Los Angeles, California. I only saw my sons during alternate holidays and summer vacations.

A divorce counselor once told me, "Kids are resilient. Even if they don't see you as often as normal parents, youngsters will adapt."

Don't swallow that psycho-babble bullshit.

As a child being summarily wrenched from my friends, torn from my activities, and ripped from my home…it created a destructive pattern in me that I unwittingly inflicted upon my own children. The sad irony is that I had buried this trauma for decades until I wrote this chapter and realized how coldly I had exacted the same pattern.

Like my father, the time I should have invested in being an attentive father was, instead, spent working 100 hours a week to pursue fame and fortune.

I found what I sought, but it cost me everything I'd desired during my fragmented childhood—safety, security, and stability.

I'm an object lesson. Thank God, there is a miracle ending to this story.

By far, the most rewarding achievement of my life is that my two sons did not follow in my footsteps. They are very successful in their respective businesses and have never moved away from their mother or their in-laws. They love their wives deeply. They are attentive to their young children (my four grandkids). Both of my sons have fulfilling relationships with their lifelong friends.

Best of all, my sons have never seen a Mayflower truck.

## What's In This For You?

*I understand the gravitational pull of ambition. I also know you may be rationalizing your hard work travel as, "I'm doing all of this for my family." Let's be honest. You're making this move for you. You want a better car. You want a bigger house. Your family doesn't care about that. Your family wants you to be present and available. If you absolutely must pack up your family and move far away, include them in the decision. Make them feel safe by showing that you care about their feelings, too.*

# CHAPTER 4

# Seek Truth

*By Allison Dalvit*

## Why Read This Story?

*You may often make life decisions based upon what you read or hear from "trusted news sources" (TV, radio, social media, hearsay). How can you be sure you are getting truthful, useful information? This story will help you sort out fact from fiction.*

My news vehicle slowed to a creep as we reached an unlit, dirt road.

Suddenly a man dressed in black appeared in my headlights, his hand was raised in the STOP position. I rolled down the driver side window to reveal the face of an angry man. "What the hell are you doing here?" He said.

Two or three other uniformed men were all but blinding us with their flashlights.

We were in trouble and I was thrilled.

The tip was right.

The ATF's presence meant there was a story. (ATF = Alcohol, Tobacco, and Firearms).

They were looking for guns.

*The scene was outside Waco, Texas. The year was 1993.*

At that time, I was every bit the stereotype of a young news reporter you've seen in the movies. Think Courtney Cox in *Scream* meets Julia Roberts in *Erin Brockovich*. I was ambitious, hungry, and stupid enough to insert myself into danger.

One Saturday night, I was working in the newsroom when I overheard our sound engineer talking about a lead he got from the local mailman. Something was happening at the Branch Davidian compound, about 12 minutes away. Without hearing more, I grabbed my weatherman. When we got to Mount Carmel, we were met by the less-than-welcoming ATF agents.

Angry Man #1 said, "Get out of the car."

I wasn't one stitch afraid.

My media pass was my superhero mask—danger couldn't touch me so long as I was with the press. I stepped out of the driver's seat; at once I was pushed up against the amateur-painted NBC logo of the news vehicle.

The agent frisked me, whisper-shouting, "Why are you here? What are you delivering to the compound?"

I kept cool, "We are with NBC news from the Waco department. I have a press badge."

Adrenaline surged in my veins. We were breaking the news! By comparison, my weatherman was sobbing with fear on the other side of the hood. I flashed my media badge and the ATF let us go. Uniform #2 walked away, "Get your asses out of here."

Ballsy Allison pried, "Can you tell us any details on what's…"

"Get. The. Hell. Out. Now!"

This kind of response is catnip to a young reporter. Something big was happening here, and I was going to be the one to break it. Hustling back to KCEN, we got our news director looped in. She encouraged me to stay on the story. She didn't need to hustle me. I was a young news hound gnawing on her first big bone.

The very next day a deadly shootout happened.

Waco is a small town where news travels fast. I felt burned that our competition broke the news before I could. I had no notion this thing would escalate at light speed.

David Koresh's followers had shot at the ATF.

Or, did they?

"Who shot who first?" …is still a matter of debate. All we knew was that shots had been fired and war was declared.

For the next 51 days the standoff was a media circus.

Federal authorities restricted us media types from the action. Imagine a never-ending line of satellite news trucks, all cameras pointed toward a building about two football fields away.

At 5 pm, everyone did a live update shot. All other times we melted in the sun, waiting for any morsel of official information. At rare FBI press briefings, we were told the Branch Davidians had a large cache of weaponry. Authorities wanted the media to know they were "a crazy and dangerous cult that was planning something."

News crews kept arriving. The FBI and ATF forces got larger. The FBI resorted to psych-ops and started flashing lights and playing decibel-shattering sounds at the compound. With as much "negotiating" that appeared to be going on, no one understood why the Branch Davidians wouldn't just come out.

And now, battle-level military equipment was being staged?

I was in the KCEN control room when one of our live TV monitors showed an army tank puncture the west wall of the compound. I raced to my news vehicle to get to the compound. In just 45 minutes, the building had caught fire and burned to the ground.

How could that have happened so quickly?!

To force the Branch Davidians out of their compound, the FBI used military-grade weaponry—and punched through the compound walls, with armored tanks, to inject tear gas. A fire broke out. The source of which remains disputed. Did the Branch Davidians start the fire? Was the FBI responsible for initiating the blaze? Were the cult members trying to escape the crumbling building? Or, were they huddling in a mass suicide mission? Regardless of circumstances or blame, 76 Branch Davidians died in the fire; among them were 25 children, two pregnant women, and David Koresh.

We were led to believe the cult had decided to die together instead of being taken captive. You cannot unsee the destruction of a compound like this. I sat staring at the ashes in a conflicted feeling of horror and relief that the story was finally over.

In the subsequent days, I stopped watching the news. I wasn't sleeping. I couldn't witness anything else. I shot everything through the viewfinder to build a barrier between what I was reporting and myself. I had gotten my big break, and I hated what the Waco experience had done to me. I surrendered my press badge.

Two decades later, after multiple anniversary reports, re-examining the standoff, new case information revealed the massive pool of reporters had been spoon-fed scripted information by the FBI.

The truth about the Waco siege made me sick all over again. I didn't know the FBI had tapes from eyewitnesses inside the compound, or that the military tank had caused the only exit to collapse, or that the tear gas was proven to be highly flammable. I trusted the FBI. I truly believed I was reporting the most accurate information to an eager public. Now I see how a government agency had written a false narrative to cover up their blunders. Unwittingly, I contributed to the dehumanization of a group of victims because I was paid to deliver "news" from the sources I was trained to trust.

## What's In This For You?

*It is increasingly harder to discern real news from social commentary...or worse...biased propaganda. Question what you are told. Fact-check what you read—and where it comes from. Then, before you jump in to endorse a story, make sure you know two things, "Who are the Villains?" and "Who are the Heroes?"*

*During the deadly Waco siege, I was a one-woman-crew (shooting, editing, writing, and reporting news stories) for KCEN, the NBC affiliate in Waco, Texas.*

*For 51 days, this was an international story that attracted dozens of TV stations, as well as all of the major networks. We all watched in horror when the compound burned to the ground.*

# CHAPTER 5

# Expect Accidents

*By Ross Shafer*

## Why Read These Stories?

*Have your good intentions ever gone sideways because you couldn't control the actions of others? Consider these next three stories as a Red Alert for how to best deal with a moment you couldn't possibly predict.*

STORY ONE: Since the days of P.T. Barnum, audiences have paid to see sideshow entertainers do mouth-dropping stunts.

At the risk of weight shaming, I am compelled to tell you that, when I was a stand-up comedian, my opening act in Sparks, Nevada, was, by far, the largest female I'd ever worked with.

Only 37, she was much taller than any of us men, wore gaudy costumes, and was so enormous, that when she walked, the stage beneath her shook. Every night, the audience gasped— then applauded when Big Bertha lumbered through the red curtain at John Ascuaga's Nugget Hotel and Casino.

Standing nine-feet tall and over 8,000 pounds you couldn't believe your eyes.

I first worked with Bertha the Elephant when I was hired

to co-headline with The Mamas & the Papas singing group ("California Dreamin'," "Monday Monday").

I'd seen Bertha's billboards after leaving the Reno airport, so I was anxious to meet her.

As soon as I got to the 1,600-room hotel, I went to the 1,000-seat showroom to see the stage manager, Geno. The rundown was this. "It's a pretty typical set up, we start at eight-sharp, Bertha goes on, does a tight-nine, and then you're up."

There was nothing typical about this!

An 8,000+ pound elephant does a tight nine-minute act? She closes her set by rearing up on her hind legs (13 feet in the air), leaves the stage—and barely squeezes by me as she exits (resembling a moving gray wall)—and now I calmly go out and do my act?

There's more. The hotel was training Bertha's replacement. "Tina" was a 1,500-pound cantankerous teenage elephant who stepped on people and broke everything in her path.

The first two nights of the six-night run were great. Clock-work perfect.

Geno came to me on the third night. "Uh, a heads up. Bertha has had a lot of indigestion due to the barley we got from Silver City so we may cut her act short."

You can tell when an 8,000-pound elephant is having gas-trointestinal issues. She can't keep up with her "Elephant Walk" calliope soundtrack. The trainer was doing her best to move Bertha into position but her hind quarter "lift" barely left the ground. Bertha took a low bow at 5 ½ minutes and turned toward the curtain.

As the curtain drew behind her, the crowd erupted in applause.

Backstage, Bertha's constipation relaxed. She broke more than wind. It was a hurricane.

When an elephant eats and (expels) 2,000 pounds of wheat and barley each day, she can manufacture a dusty, olive-colored fog! I could barely see. Stagehands cleaned up the mess while Geno turned on an aircraft fan to dissipate the fog. On cue, the band "played Bertha off" so the audience couldn't hear the pachyderm explosion behind me.

Not that you would know this, but an elephant fart is long and deep—sounds like the U.S. Navy has docked!

Amidst the pandemonium, I heard the stage announcer say, "Ladies and Gentlemen, the comedy stylings of Mr. Ross Shafer." I went through the curtain, followed by the dusty olive fog and the wafting stench.

People were turning their heads in a collective wince. All eyes in the first three rows were watering. Some of the audience thought I was the cause. Others knew this had to be from a nearby circus animal.

I couldn't have predicted this. But I was responsible for dealing with the unexpected consequences that were threatening my job.

I waited until the music stopped and said, "I love this hotel… but you know that Mexican Buffet just off the lobby? (pause) Don't go back for SECONDS!" Then, I did the hold-my-stomach-fake-burp gesture.

I took "the blame" and my absurd exaggeration was the perfect segue for a once-in-a-lifetime awkward circumstance.

BTW: Bertha was fine for the rest of the run.

Whenever your job is dependent upon a "group" reaction,

you can predict if something can go wrong—it will go wrong. How will you pivot when "the unforeseeable" is lurking to derail your goals?

STORY TWO: Several years into my comedy career I had become very confident in my act. I had jokes that worked every time, for every audience—or so I thought.

In 1984, I was hired for what, to me, was a fortune ($5,000). I would be the "middle act" for two famous rock bands at the Washington State Fair.

The band Steppenwolf ("Born to be Wild," "Magic Carpet Ride," "The Pusher") would do a 30-minute set, I'd go out and tell jokes for 20 minutes, while the band Three Dog Night ("Never Been to Spain," "Joy to the World," "Mama Told me Not to Come") cleared the Steppenwolf gear and set up their own instruments behind me.

In minutes, it was a total disaster in front of 8,000 screaming fans.

Steppenwolf shot to fame for being a huge part of the *Easy Rider* movie soundtrack.

Consequently, Steppenwolf drew a dangerous biker crowd… as in the Hell's Angels and The Vagos. My preppy Coogi sweater was the wrong outfit. My tame jokes about growing up in the suburbs bombed. My once-brazen confidence shriveled like jumping into a cold shower.

I was booed.

I was cat-called.

Ten minutes into my twenty, I turned to see if Three Dog Night might be ready, early.

Their road manager pulled his arms up to his throat to give me the universal S-T-R-E-T-C-H sign.

Nightmare continued.

Under my breath, I uttered, "I'm not getting paid enough for this shit." But, of course, there is no such thing as "under your breath" when your mouth is close to a stadium quality microphone! The audience heard me and started hurling silver coins at me. Quarters, dimes, and nickels pelted me like iron rain for the next 15 minutes.

Three Dog Night gave me the thumbs up and my final words to the angry throng were me shouting at the top of my range, "Ladies and gentlemen, the band you have been waiting for… THREE! DOG! NIGHT!"

The arena's din was deafening.

My job was done. So was my career.

I felt so ashamed. I just wanted out of there. As I scurried down the back stairs, I was stopped by Three Dog Night's manager. "Ross? Or… is it Russ? Hey man, I heard the thunder when you announced the band. You must be killer! Nobody's ever lasted that long. Please, come on tour with us!"

Sometimes, when you think extenuating circumstances (out of your control) have destroyed your chances of achieving your goals, you're wrong. We can't always perceive the truth others see. Wait until the final outcome before you judge yourself.

STORY THREE: When a comedian does well 'opening the show' for a famous singer or band, it is likely they will get a lot of work on tour with them.

I got a call to be an emergency fill-in act for singer Crystal

Gayle ("Don't it Make your Brown Eyes Blue?" and "Have You Left the Woman You Left Me For?"). Having worked with Diana Ross and Dionne Warwick, I knew my higher energy would complement Crystal's gentle style.

The first concert went well. Her husband/manager Bill Gatzimos hired me to follow them to Caesar's Palace in Las Vegas. Offstage, Bill and Crystal liked me and I had a feeling this was going to be a long-term run.

Crystal was beautiful and audiences loved her. She was barely five feet tall, tiny, and her signature "look" was her silky floor-length brown hair. While she used her locks effectively as a swinging prop in her act, it must have taken days to dry.

The first night, I went out to a crowd of 1,200 and killed it. Every joke worked and I could see Bill in the wings laughing hard. I finished, took a bow, and went backstage to meet Crystal and Bill.

Before Crystal took the stage, her band played a three-minute number to hype the crowd for Crystal's arrival. It was customary for the headliner to ask the opening act (ME) "How's the mood of the house?" "Are there any super fans?" In the darkened wings of the theater, I was standing close enough to her to whisper all good things.

The announcer blared, "PLEASE WELCOME...CRYSTAL GAYLE!"

She said, "See you later honey," and kissed her husband.

Crystal began to move elegantly into the curtain's spotlight... when her head snapped back in full whiplash!

I WAS STANDING ON HER HAIR!

Bill went crazy! Crystal screamed! I got fired!

I completely understood why her husband was furious. I blew her beautifully choreographed and graceful entrance. I was the unforeseeable contingency!

I never worked with them again.

Sometimes, unexpected consequences that short-circuit our goals are caused by our own actions. All you can do is take ownership, apologize, and try to avoid repeating a mistake. In my case, I have never been hired by anyone with floor length hair since.

## What's In This For You?

*Life has a way of going wrong at any moment. Prepare for it if you can. If you can't, face the consequences head on and develop a short-term memory so you can move on.*

*Stepping on Crystal's 62" brown mane of hair cost me a tour with her. She was a sweetheart. I was a liability.*

SHOW BIZ TIP: Never work in close quarters with a pachyderm in gastrointestinal pain.

# CHAPTER 6

# Love Deeply

*By Allison Dalvit*

## Why Read This Story?

*The great enemy of love is lost time. If you have ever regretted choosing work or hobbies over precious time with a loved one, I hope this story realigns your priorities.*

I don't love part-time. If I love you, I submerge myself. My love engulfs; it floods and overflows. I don't love in gallons. I love in oceans, in fathoms that plummet to the unknown sea beds. Flowery and dramatic, I know. I went overboard—yeah, another seafaring reference—but it's so you will get the point. I love deeply.

I gained this sensibility from my dad. He taught me to honor love's capacity and resilience, even as his own body was betraying him.

Heart disease leeched his life for over 40 years. My father's heart first attacked him at age 35.

After his first cardiac episode, Dad was so terrified of death, he taught me how to drive a stick shift. Never mind that I didn't have a valid license. I was only 8. But my age was of no disquiet to my engineer father as he was used to using multipliers of two when either building a bridge span or having his life expectancy halved. Al Dalvit wasn't about to die without his daughter knowing how to wheel him to the ER in his 1969 Ford F100. I couldn't reach the pedals, but he was confident I would solve that. My dad also taught me resuscitation techniques and the secret location of his "magic pill" (front left jeans pocket). People who love deeply memorize where the nitroglycerine stash lives.

He didn't just rely on my "salad days" driving skills, or the life-saving nitro, Dad was thorough. He had a spiritual insurance policy. For 46 years, Dad wore a gold St. Christopher medallion around his neck, a token my mom gave him when they got engaged. He never took it off unless he was getting a dental X-ray, or he was having major heart surgery. The few times Dad took the necklace off, he ceremoniously sited it around my neck, telling me, "I'll be back for my St. Chris after surgery. Take care of it for me, Ali. You are my lucky charm!"

Trustworthiness is the recompense for loving deeply.

That ritual happened countless times. But at 74, Dad had exhausted his allowance of heartbeats. Much of his blood pump had calcified.

With about ten percent function remaining, the doctors shuddered to tell me my father would only have a scant eight weeks left to draw breath.

Dad absorbed this headline with his typical resolve. He looked at me and said, "Let's go home."

Home side, he sank into his two-decade-old Lay-Z-Boy rocker, surrounded by framed photos of his family, his classic car models, and the large bearskin named "Booger" he had guarding his bedroom hallway. The recliner was where Dad spent the most amount of his time, watching sports or making labels on his label maker; it soon became where he would undergo his daily regimen of three-dozen complex, sequential meds, administered by (sorely under-qualified) me. The oxygen man rang his doorbell often to top off a clown-sized tank. The cistern was tethered by a fifty-foot-long cord so Dad could wander between rooms. Heartbreaking was the day Dad convened my brother and I into his living room to apprise us of his living will. We were in our 40s, yet my father's "Affairs in Order Speech" made us feel like children.

My brother stared into space. I couldn't stop sobbing.

Awaiting death overhauls your priorities. Seeing the reality of my dad's short time on earth convinced me to exchange a promising reality TV casting director job for the blessing to clock in as his 24/7 duty nurse.

We had fun!

We watched the Colorado Rockies play baseball and we tended to his garden. We made homemade fruit popsicles (he had no appetite for real food). Usually followed by tripping off to his daily doctor appointments. I was his designated "pill buddy," the keeper of the mountain of medications.

To say we "bonded" over this, shames the word. We had loved each other deeply for a lifetime; and his needing me now completed the circle. Although his cardiac organ only performed at 10%, Dad loved with the capacity of a heart in full beat.

One morning I went to check on him, and I couldn't tell if he was breathing. His chest was no longer rising. In a panic, I jumped into his bed and clutched onto him as if he was dangling from an icy ledge. He gasped and started breathing again. I will never forget the fear I saw on his face. He knew he was dying. And soon. He had been a tremendous father and grandfather. I had to let him know how valuable he was to me. It was my chance to affirm how thankful I was for everything he gave me. For a beautiful childhood. For the indelible life lessons. For the spectacular experiences he'd provided for me. We both cried and held onto each other for as long as possible before his 10 a.m. doctor appointment.

We were mostly quiet on the drive back. I reckon that my father was confronting his fate. He broke the silence with,

"Ali, there's something crucial I want to share with you." I knew the tone well enough to stiffen.

"Ok…I'm ready."

"I want a WHOPPPPAAA," He said.

What?! He hadn't had an appetite in weeks.

I laughed out loud. "A WHOPPPAAA?!?"

"Yes! A WHOPPPAAA!"

We repeated the word until we magically summoned a Burger King. In the parking lot, we donned paper Burger King crowns and made jokes with mouthfuls of meat. The Whopper actually normalized life, for a bit.

This would be Dad's last meal.

The next day when I pulled up to his house, I saw three emergency vehicles in a full light show. I flew out of my car to the already open door. My aunt intercepted me in the living room: "I was knocking on the front door and heard a loud thump." Dad never locked his door, so my aunt walked in and found my father on the kitchen floor. 911 was her first call.

When I got to the kitchen, the paramedics were already in the third act of trying to save my father's life. The defibrillator paddles were bouncing against my father's chest; until I leaned down to stop them, "If you're getting a heartbeat, it's from his pacemaker."

They stood down. A hero's effort, but it was over.

Love doesn't fail—hearts do.

When the paramedics left, I stayed on the kitchen floor with Dad. I propped his head on a pillow, delicately wrapped him in a blanket, draped my arm over his chest and held onto him for a long time. It was the final and sweetest goodbye.

Eight hours passed.

I only know that because that's how long it took the mortuary to get the clearance to pick him up.

As they rolled his body away, I transferred Dad's Saint Christopher necklace from his neck to mine for the last time. It's been seven years. I've never taken St. Chris off.

To this day, people still ask me, "Did you know you were with him on the kitchen floor for eight hours?" I didn't. There is no stopwatch on love. It is important to take our time with our loved ones, for those are the moments when time should stand still.

## What's In This For You?

*When somebody would tell me, "The greatest gift you can give someone is your time," I would roll my eyes. But I get it now. You will never regret giving a little more time to the person who has very little of it left.*

*Deep love for my hero, my protector, my Dad.*

*Dad worked hard and played harder.*

*Dad loved to drive his Model T Ford in the annual Breckenridge 4th of July parade. Riding shotgun is his granddaughter, Cass.*

# CHAPTER 7

# Stop Guilt

*By Ross Shafer*

### Why Read This Story?

*Have you ever won a big job or scored a financial windfall that you didn't feel you deserved? Me Too! My hope is that this story will recalibrate your brain so you can release your guilt.*

People die and I benefit.

This has happened too many times over the years.

I thought by admitting it in print I'd be able to purge the guilt—but the truth of it makes me feel worse.

I first became a television star because a man named Al Wallace died and left a half hour time slot open on Sunday nights.

During the 1970's and 1980's Al Wallace hosted the long-running TV magazine show *How Come* on Seattle's KING-TV. The show covered topics on how things were made—and how things were done in the world. As a kid, I watched it every week; always learned something cool.

Fast forward fifteen years. Al Wallace dies.

Al's death motivated KING-TV to develop a replacement for

*How Come.* I had become a respectable stand-up comedian and was out doing "guest shots" on talk shows.

I was a guest on the Alan Thicke talk show in Canada when KING's promo and marketing director, Pat Cashman, saw me and suggested I be considered to take over Al's time slot.

I was called in and offered the chance to create a comedy talk show (later titled, *Almost Live!*). *Almost Live!* won 100+ local and national awards. We generated international publicity (some good, some bad) and sold millions of dollars in beer and auto advertising during its 15-year run.

Thanks to *Almost Live!* my professional life was sustained for 35+ years, all because kindly old Al Wallace expired.

It would be one thing if that happened to me once—but due to the death of somebody, my career has been advanced two more times.

After 4 ½ years as the creator and host of *Almost Live!*, I was mustered to Hollywood (by the Fox Network) to host their nightly comedy/talk show, *The Late Show*.

I landed the host position because FOX had a beef with their original host, Joan Rivers. The story, as it was told to me by a segment producer, was that Joan's husband Edgar Rosenberg was over-meddling in the minutiae of the show. 20th Century FOX president, Barry Diller, lost his patience and asked Edgar to leave. Joan defended her husband and accompanied him out the door.

Once away from the studio, Joan and Edgar separated. My sources claimed that FOX was negotiating a sort of 'save face' posture for Joan to return. Sadly, Edgar was so depressed at being fired (and separated from his wife) that he committed suicide. Joan was too distraught to work.

After a nationwide search for a replacement host, I got the job.

Again, I got promoted as a result of someone else dying.

Did I feel guilty? YES!

In the back of my mind, I knew I wouldn't have landed this high-profile job if Edgar Rosenberg were still alive.

*The Late Show* was cancelled eight months later.

The national exposure from that highly publicized late-night show (which competed against Johnny Carson's *Tonight Show*) gave me the credibility to audition for other network TV shows.

Luckily, I was hired to move to New York City where I co-hosted an ABC network late-night talk and magazine show *Day's End* produced by SQuire Rushnell, the man who put *Good Morning America* in first place. SQuire was also a father of *Schoolhouse Rock* and created *The Kingdom Chums*. I shared the *Day's End* stage with Spencer Christian, Matt Lauer, Hanna Storm, and Diana Nyad. After six months, we were cancelled— and I went back to my home in Los Angeles.

One night, I was watching the 6 o'clock news.

I sat shocked to hear, Bert Convy, one of TV's most likable actors and game show hosts (*Super Password, Win, Lose, or Draw, Tattletales*) had died of a brain tumor. Bert was only 57.

The next day, I got a call from my agent at William Morris asking me to audition for "that game show Bert Convy was slated to host."

That's Hollywood for you…the casket wasn't even in the ground and some agent was lining up a new, warm body.

I was the warm body.

I went through the paces for one of the world's greatest game show icons, Mark Goodson, of Goodson-Todman Productions, which created and produced *The Price is Right, Family Feud, Card Sharks, I've Got a Secret,* and *What's My Line?*

In the wake of Bert's death, Goodson was now recasting his 70's hit, *Match Game.*

Mark Goodson couldn't have been nicer, for a guy in a hurry.

He had a one-year contract to produce *Match Game* for the ABC network and he had to find another host—pronto. The host selection process came down to two of us—Vicki Lawrence and me. I got the job.

For the third time in my life, I benefitted from the death of a really nice person.

I felt guilty and lucky at the same time.

This pattern has happened outside of my professional career.

I received a modest inheritance when my mother died. I felt guilty thinking, "I don't deserve this money. I didn't earn a penny of this."

Good fortune found me even when no money was involved. I met and fell in love with my fiancé only because her ex-husband unexpectedly died.

This array was really starting to screw with my head. I wondered if I would have been worthy of these extraordinary prosperities if all of these people were still alive.

I'll tell you who and what finally assuaged my guilt.

Fifteen years after I'd co-hosted *Day's End* for ABC, producer and friend, SQuire Rushnell, he and his world-class comic impressionist wife, Louise DuArt, finally quelled my guilt.

They had written a series of 12 very successful and insightful books called *Godwinks*, except for one called *Dogwinks*. You can imagine what that's about.

The accredited definition of a Godwink is: an event or personal experience, often identified as coincidence, so astonishing that it is seen as a sign of divine intervention, especially when perceived as the answer to a prayer.

This explanation dissolved all guilt for me.

I used to accept my good luck as a coincidence, a matter of galactic timing. But these opportunties happened too often for them to be mere chance. The confluence of these events was nothing short of ... astonishing. The timing of a door closing on one life—and simultaneously opening up for me—felt unfair. I made jokes that it was 'destiny.' I was parroting what I heard other people say, "The stars just lined up."

By SQuire and Louise's definition, what was happening to me was "Star-Like...a Divine Alignment," as SQuire would say. I am a dedicated man of faith, so I began to look at my life through that lens. Everything that had happened to me could be traced back to my practice of dutifully praying for it to happen. (SQuire and Louise reminded me to keep doing that.)

Uh oh, I suspect I've alienated the atheists. No hard feelings. Let's talk about YOU.

If you suspect a higher power exists—whether you're a Christian, a Catholic, a Protestant, Muslim, Jewish, Hindu, "The Secret" Spiritualist, or a Buddhist, then you have probably attributed some unexplainable event in your life to something other than a coincidence—something greater than your own understanding.

So, why was I burdened with guilt in the first place?

I felt guilty because I was sharing the responsibility of another person's demise. Instead of letting God drive the bus, I made the fatal flaw of thinking I was rewiring His GPS in my favor.

That's the height of arrogance.

I am finally convinced I'm not in control…never was. I trust I was exactly where I was supposed to be when my miracles happened. I believe a higher power nudges the course corrections in our lives because we are finally prepared to carry the torch to the next leg of the journey.

It's also not a coincidence that some of you needed to read this chapter.

## What's In This For You?

*Does it disturb you to think that maybe your life is just a series of random coincidences? Have you ever left your home two minutes late only to learn you avoided a deadly car accident? Then, maybe you can entertain the idea that you are not in charge of the world.*

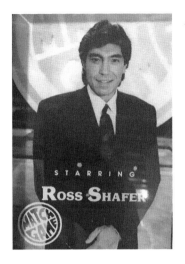

MATCH GAME was rebooted
in 1990 with host Bert Convy.
When Bert died I auditioned
and won the job.

After Joan Rivers was let go by
the FOX-TV network, her husband took his own life. After two
dozen well known personalities
auditioned, I was given the permanent job on April 7, 1988.

I got the job of creating a replacement show after the death of
TV host, Al Wallace. Al hosted
KING-TV's "How Come?" for a
dozen years.

# CHAPTER 8

# Believe Intuition

*By Allison Dalvit*

## Why Read This Story?

*If you don't use your pre-birth intuition and instincts, they will atrophy. Don't believe you have those traits? Think about the inexplicable connection you have with your child. Has it ever been so strong that you've had a bad feeling about their safety when they weren't with you? This story will convince you to trust those feelings.*

I was a tomboy.

At least, that's what other people called me.

Now that I think about it, I was never heralded as being "all sugar and spice and everything nice."

I was better known as fiercely independent.

I was the first and only girl on the all-boy's T-ball team.

I was a daredevil who liked to ride dirt bikes.

I was an acrobatic snow skier.

I was that kid who would perform dangerous stunts if I thought I could make people laugh.

As I got older, the tomboy in me realized that boys were

starting to get cuter. Did I ever confess this to my mom? No! I was too embarrassed to talk about this boy crazy evolution with either of my parents. Besides, I wanted to check out the scene first, just in case my hormonal reactions were caused by too much sugar.

When two of the most popular boys in elementary school asked me and Carol (my best friend) to meet them at Chatfield Lake, I was pretty excited. Chatfield was a wonderland of fun— and this sounded like a moment to garner some derring-do attention.

So, for our first "date," Carol and I rode our bikes to the lake.

It was a chilly winter in Colorado. It was easy to see the lake was frozen solid.

When we spotted the boys, I knew they would like me if I went straight for the laughs.

Elementary school comedy meant me riding my bike out onto the ice, slipping, sliding, and poppin' wheelies.

The boys were a great audience, and I was a hit.

Since they witnessed my X-Games-like exhibition on the frozen surface, the boys challenged all of us to walk all the way across the lake. It was probably half a mile...maybe more. We threw our bikes on the shore and started our ice-walking.

Forty feet from the shore, my foot fell through the ice.

My wet foot became even funnier joke material. I'm waving my arms over my head in a mock display of imbalance.

But in my head, I was thinking maybe the lake wasn't totally frozen? I can't remember if it was Carol or myself who suggested we'd better head back to the shore.

On our walk back, every now and again, one of our feet would crunch through the ice. (meaning the ice was less than two inches thick). I'm the fearless adventurer but even I knew this quest was no longer funny.

I started to panic. I pretended to have this situation under control, but I truly had no idea what to do. As a sixth grader, I weighed less than 80 pounds and with every step I was cracking the ice. In school, I'd learned that for an ice sheet to crust over two inches, the water underneath has to be 40 degrees below zero. If I fell in, nobody could save me before hypothermia would take me down.

Then, I heard my mother's voice hollering from the shore.

"Allison! ALLISON!"

She was screaming for us to "spread out and walk back s-l-o-w-l-y!"

We took her advice and spread out so we wouldn't be putting too much weight on one spot. She pushed the frame of my bike onto the lake, front wheel first so I had something to grab.

But how did she even know we were there?! And how did she know to look at this spot in 11 miles of shoreline?

I didn't tell anyone we were going to Chatfield Lake. At this time in the history of telecommunications, there were no cell phones, no GPS, and no tracking devices.

My mom just had a hunch and instinctively drove to the lake because, somehow, she knew her child was in danger.

Afterward, out of all the places I was allowed to go, Mom couldn't explain her inner urge to look for us at the lake.

She didn't question her intuition. She got in her car and drove to me.

It was a miracle the evening news wasn't reporting that four kids were found dead under a frozen lake.

I never kept anything from my mother, ever again.

With her internal homing device, she would know what I was up to anyway!

As I was writing this story I wanted to know if a mother's intuition was simply a coincidence with me or if other moms felt this kind of clairvoyance.

Dr. Victor Shamas, a psychologist at the University of Arizona, believes mothers have an innate sixth sense. "When a woman is pregnant and the mother and child share one body, it must somehow facilitate some sort of intersubjective connection."

Michelle Mathis, of Cardiff by the Sea, CA, told www.Today.com that, during a family party, she felt a strange urge to find her two-year-old daughter, Delia. Mrs. Mathis last saw Delia playing in the yard, fully clothed, yet without seeing her daughter she instinctively dove into the swimming pool, found Delia underwater, and rescued her. She was amazed at the tragedy she had prevented by acting on her innate instincts.

Have you had an instinct-only episode happen to you? If so, we'd love for you to tell us about it on our website. (https://rossshafer.com/topics/rattled-how-to-go-from-shook-to-solid/)

## What's In This For You?

*Yes, technology can track our children via cell phones. But I'm afraid our 'digital dependence' may be dulling our natural intuitive powers. Instead of searching Google or WebMD for "the right answers," pay attention to your inner siren when it blares, "I have a bad feeling about this." That's your intuition telling you something Doctor Internet cannot.*

*Mom and me. Her intuitive connection started this early and has grown every day since.*

# CHAPTER 9

# Rehearse Life

*By Ross Shafer*

## Why Read This Story?

*Have you ever given the wrong answer at the wrong time, causing yourself humiliation and embarrassment? Then maybe you should practice how you think.*

You don't have all the answers.

In fact, you might live in fear of being asked a tricky question at work.

What if you draw a blank and a wrong answer casts a dark shadow on your future?

Or, how about this? Your mate wants you to clarify something dumb you uttered. But you honestly can't remember what you said. A random guess could be catastrophic and further strain your relationship.

Life is littered with unexpected scenarios where you are expected to say the right thing at the right time. A good answer makes you appear wise and thoughtful. Articulation causes other people to trust your judgment.

Too often we fail.

We all know the feeling of *"I wish I had said......."*

The perfect afterthought occurs to us long after the prime window of delivery.

Political comedian, Mort Sahl, was often asked for his election prognostications. Mort said, "I wish to reserve my judgment until I can render hindsight."

When you are asked difficult questions, you are wise to remember these three words: Don't wing it!

My lesson in "No Winging" happened when I took over *The Late Show* from Joan Rivers. The stakes on a network talk show were incredibly high. FOX spent millions of dollars to attract millions of viewers. Dumb errors by their host were not tolerated.

Immediately, I was enrolled into a kind of "talk show school."

My first day on the job started at 8 a.m. Coming from the Number 13th ranked Seattle TV market, I was pretty excited to be playing in the Major Leagues.

My enthusiasm was tempered when I met three somber executive producers who got in my face, "You are going to have the biggest stars and world shakers on your couch each night. You'll have to create instant rapport with your guests so they will open up to you. When that happens, we want you to ask them the toughest questions imaginable. We want to make news. That's not all. At any time, up to 375 reporters from newspapers, radio stations, and local TV stations from around the country will be trying to get you to screw up on the record. They will ask you why you deserve this job. They will quiz you about how smart and funny you are. We need you to sound well-informed, intelligent, and appropriately glib."

O K A Y, I got the message. This was how the Big Time does business. No element of the show was left to chance, especially my parts.

My day went like this:

From 9 a.m. to noon, I would work with seven joke writers. All of us would dissect every possible news source to find topical news stories we could skewer. I'd get about 100 jokes to choose from. From that bucket I'd pick six to nine to fill a seven-minute opening monologue.

At 1 p.m., stage rehearsals with visiting musical acts and/or comedians would happen. Bands were usually grumpy and demanding. Comedians were grateful and nervous.

From 2-3 p.m., I met with each of four segment producers to get a list of pre-approved questions for each of my guests. The segment producers had already spent 45 minutes on the phone with a guest and the probing questions we chose would cue the guest to tell their (hopefully) amusing/revealing three-minute story—to plug their book or tell a tale about making their new movie. I couldn't believe I was about to become "friends" with these famous people, so I worked at becoming an ardent fan during my hour.

From 3-4 p.m., I would meet with the comedy writers a second time to brainstorm ad-libs for each guest's interview. (Ad-libs are pre-written funny comments I could throw in if the interview was drowning). Most of the ad-libs wouldn't be allowed for TV...but OMG I never laughed harder.

From 4-4:45 p.m. was wardrobe, makeup, and a brief hello to the arriving guests. Each guest had a beautiful private dressing room—and each one received a boxed set of wine and glasses. Guests were generally more entertaining if they drank.

We taped the show from 5-6 p.m. and sent the feed to New York for its 11:30 p.m. airing.

Once we were done taping, from 6:00-6:45 p.m., I would go back to my office, eat a little dinner, and watch the show we just recorded. TV is the great equalizer. The shows that absolutely rocked somehow weren't as good on TV. The shows that stunk in the studio remarkably looked just fine on TV. Regardless, every show could have been improved.

From 7-8 p.m., I would meet with my current affairs squad— not the TV show but my culture update team.

Two young researchers would get me up to speed on significant pop culture celebrities, music, politics, fashion, medicine, as well as any goofy trends I should know about (like the Teenage Mutant Ninja Turtle phenomenon).

Why go through this tedious process every night? Because the "What's Hot? What's Not?" list would often shift overnight. I had to be able to comment with awareness (on stage or in a press interview) as if I was "in the know" about everything, at any moment. Together, we would all write my answers and I'd go away to rehearse them.

My nightly prep wasn't over yet.

From 8-9 p.m., I'd go into a windowless office and hone my press conference skills. I never gave one press conference… but still…

When you see any press conference on TV, the "star" has been well prepped. In my case, an associate producer would ask me a series of random questions I might be asked by a reporter. After all, I'm representing the FOX Network and I wanted to make certain the executives and all of our affiliates were proud of my answers.

Again, I'd write and rehearse my answers so I could sound alert, quick, bright, funny, or somber, depending upon the tone of the question. Some examples:

"Over 200 people auditioned for this job. How did you get it?

"What makes you think you can make a dent in Johnny Carson's ratings?"

"You are currently losing to Ted Koppel's *Nightline*. How can you beat him?"

"You recently visited the Playboy Mansion. What impressed you there?"

"Is that your real hair?

"You wear a wedding ring, but we have never seen your wife. Does she exist?"

"Who has been your most interesting guest?"

"Who has been your worst guest?"

"How does it feel when your jokes bomb during the monologue?"

"You make a lot of jokes about the President. Are you a democrat?"

"Do you remember where you were when Martin Luther King was shot?"

I'd get home to my Burbank apartment about 10:30 p.m., eat a low-calorie desert (chocolate frozen yogurt was my fav), and trudge to my home office to study any notes for the next day's show.

The practice of preparing my answers and rehearsing my responses has become a lifelong habit. Pre-thinking my responses to predictable questions has saved me an ocean of perspiration and stress over the years.

If you want to appear smarter, wiser, and more articulate (in any circumstance) I urge you to intentionally make an exhaustive list of the questions people at work might ask you. Make a list of all the questions your children will ask you. Make a list of as many questions you think your mate might ask you.

Once you have your lists, rehearse your answers over and over. Don't assume you will be wise, bright, and appropriate on demand. Nobody is that smart.

If you don't prepare, you will have regrets. However, preparation will always reward you.

Some of you are already accustomed to prepping - and you don't even realize it. You organize and file tasty recipes you want to repeat. You're planning ahead. You watch YouTube videos on how to fix your plumbing. You're practicing. You try to remember your favorite jokes so you can re-tell them to friends. You are memorizing.

Don't wing answering questions. Most questions have the potential for making you look like an idiot. Don't wing big decisions in a pressure-sensitive moment. Decide ahead of time.

Prepare yourself for moments that allow you to show off your best self.

You never know when someone might just give you a talk show.

## What's In This For You?

*A lot of people are depending on you for the right answers. Why not meditate on how you will answer life's toughest questions? You will look like a hero for having the best solution, long before you need it.*

*On a talk show, the host's day isn't over when the curtain closes. Lots of studying for tomorrow's guests, writing "witty ad libs," and rehearsing answers for unexpected press questions. Prep is actually fun! It weirdly feels like a final exam you can't wait to take.*

# CHAPTER 10

# Kill Distractions

*By Allison Dalvit*

## Why Read This Story?

*Are you a laser-focused, goal-oriented person who refuses to stop until you get what you want? Me too. This story will encourage you to kill the distractions… before distractions kill you.*

I should have died when a red pickup truck T-boned me broadside.

Luckily, my limp 105 pounds was launched across a busy intersection.

I say "lucky" because the bike I was riding had become tangled beneath the truck's chassis and was dragged for three miles.

When my 21-year-old body left Earth, the event was happening in…s-l-o-w m-o-t-i-o-n.

Mid-air, I could have sworn a giant hand caught me like a fly ball in a kidskin glove. I truly believe that an act of God, "the hand," cushioned my fall.

That's how catechism colors you.

I landed on the hot pavement and skipped like a river stone to the other side of the street. Implausible but true, a paramedic truck was parked nearby. Everything after that was hazy.

I woke up in a hospital emergency room, surrounded by the scuttle of doctors and nurses. One nurse was scrubbing the right side of my face with an abrasive pad. I didn't feel pain—but I will never forget the smell of baby shampoo. This woman's job was to clean the "road rash" (aka the pavement particles) still embedded in my face.

I had broken bones.

Shattered molars.

My skin was shredded.

I suffered a severe head injury.

The jeans I wore were ripped in strips (this was before that look was intentional). The denim was stained red, exposing my bloody legs. I assumed the recoloring was from my blood. Closer examination indicated my jeans had absorbed crimson paint from the truck's hood.

They never caught the driver who hit me—but three miles away, the police found what was left of my bike's frame, folded in half like a ragged paperback. No sign of tires.

Piecing it all back together, I had the green walk signal—yet the entire incident was my fault.

I was totally distracted by my ambitions.

To graduate in 3 1/2 years years (with a degree in journalism) I had orchestrated a one-semester jump on my classmates. Obtaining that early diploma meant stacking my classes practically on top of one another.

To layer on more pressure, I took a full-time job as a disc jockey at Power 107.9 FM radio in Fort Collins, CO.

Driven, baby, driven!

My typical day unfurled like this:

I would do my college homework during an extended "set" of music. (A set of music would consist of 4-5 uninterrupted songs, meaning no commercials). When the set ended, I'd click back on the air, tell some jokes, update a contest, do weather or news, and introduce the next extended set of music.

When my radio shift ended at midnight, I'd pick up my drunk sorority sisters at whatever bar had beer and boys, drop them all off at the sorority house, then head back home. I'd catch a few winks and start the "class dash" early the next morning. Weekends were reserved for live radio remotes and group projects for school. It was my senior year and finals week was barreling towards me.

My singular enemy was…time. I needed to trim the fat from my days.

The answer to improving my efficiency came in the vision of a beautiful mountain bike. The one I coveted was the marquee of the Specialized brand. I stared at this sparkly blue hardtail until I spent nearly all of my radio money to take it home. The model was a "rockhopper"—the first choice of the competition crowd who jumped stumps and careened down un-groomed terrain at profane speeds.

I calculated this badass bike could cut my daily travel time by 27%--not cut by a ¼, but exactly 27%. Feeling fast and furious, I crossed a familiar intersection (without looking right or left) focused on arriving at the Clark Building ten minutes early for my finals. I would have except for…

SMACK! The Truck.

If I had not been so distracted over saving a few ticks by riding my bike to class, I could have forgone my young life's most frightening hospital visit.

I was wrong about time being my enemy. Time was what healed my wounds. Time became the best friend who taught me perspective. I am still busy and ambitious, but I can now recognize when the distraction beast is taunting me.

I was able to recover, get back to work and graduate early.

I covered the scars on my forehead with my bangs. And…I nailed down an on-air television job soon after graduation.

Still, every time I look in the mirror, pull my bangs aside, and see the scars, I'm reminded that my worst distraction was…me. I nearly got myself killed.

I'm definitely more aware of other motorists now. I actually wrangle with passengers to let me do the driving. Beyond that, I am focused on a thousand potential threats when I'm with my daughters. You know, like kidnappers hiding under cars, driving alone at night, and not engaging with aggressive road rage drivers.

While this might sound a little paranoid to you, the near-death lesson I carry with me to this day is: "Allison, look around. Ignoring danger will add more risk and erase joy."

## What's In This For You?

*Sometimes being too distracted can literally end your life (like the almost-deadly red truck). Some people say, "Just live in the moment." I say, "Notice dangerous moments."*

*This is what a "road rash" looks like when you skid your face across the busiest intersection near Colorado State University.*

# CHAPTER 11

# Be Mindful

*By Ross Shafer*

## Why Read This Story?

*We speak approximately 5,000 words a day. The tone in which we sprinkle those words can make a person feel either loved and appreciated—or dismissed and unimportant. This story is about managing the thoughts in your head, before they get blurted out as words.*

I watched a real man die…on television.

The victim insulted his attacker. Then, the attacker killed him over a single word.

As a young boy, my dad loved to corral my two brothers and me around our 21-inch black and white Philco television to watch the Gillette *Friday Night Fights*.

Dad cooked up salted puffed wheat and encouraged us to get as loud as we wanted. It was Father and Sons bonding time.

One Friday night, we were excited to watch welterweight boxing challenger Emile Griffith fight reigning champion Benny "Kid" Paret. This was their third bout, and the score was locked at one victory each.

In the first ten rounds, the champ Paret lost points to Griffith—but in the 11th, Paret knocked Griffith to the canvas. Paret wore a smug grin as he sat on his corner stool.

The bell clanged for Round 12. The boxers were exhausted right up until Griffith landed a vicious right hand to Paret's jaw. My dad said, "Uh oh, Griffith is finally mad." Griffith's fists pounded Paret with 29 consecutive blows. He just wouldn't stop! Even as Paret's unconscious body slid to the canvas, Griffith kept landing blows.

The referee finally stopped the fight, giving Griffith the TKO win and the welterweight title.

Yet, the victory wasn't a celebration.

Paret never regained consciousness and died a few days later.

We boys had a lot of questions—but our father didn't want to talk about it. We never gathered for *Friday Night Fights* again.

For weeks, sportscasters would speculate, "Why did Griffith continue to pummel Paret when he was clearly knocked out?"

A dozen years later, when I was writing a college paper, I discovered the truth.

During their weigh-in for the fight, Paret called Griffith a "maricon," which was Cuban gutter slang for "homosexual." This slur gnawed at Griffith for every waking moment up to the fight.

Once in the ring, Griffith unleashed his rage to the point of literally killing his opponent.

The consequences of One Word haunted Emile Griffith every day for the next 50 years. Griffith died from dementia on July 23, 2013.

What ferocious words have you leveled at someone in anger?

Later, were you wracked with guilt and regret?

Do you ever think about the unintended consequences of your social media posts? Hiding behind the safety of their keyboards, the vile exchanges I've seen between Facebook "friends" are insulting, degrading, disrespectful, condescending, and hateful. I call it "Page Rage" because these spineless halfwits would never direct those words face-to-face to a larger, unstable human being.

Imagine if your words were the last words your "friend" carried with them into their final moments on earth.

After my divorce, I was alone and confused by what happened. I decided to write about my experiences (somewhat shrouded) on Facebook to earnestly solicit wisdom and feedback from others.

I posted questions like, *"Do you have an enemy?" "At what point do you forgive them?" "Do you write in a journal?" "Tell us why journaling is valuable to you?"*

One Facebook "friend" (whom I didn't know personally), Julia Anne Throckmorton-Miller, was thoughtful and brutally honest.

She took my questions seriously and I always acknowledged her remarks with respect. Here is a response to my question about the value of journaling.

*When I journal, it is normally when my heart is ready to burst. I lay on my bed with no distractions. I then get my brain turned over to God. He is the one writing the words. Please protect my dog, all my children and Grandbabies. I am broken but praying God will step in. I will stop crying soon. My Mother would beat me if I ever cried so at 50. I will soon go back to hospice and sit with the dying. Their testimony is right before they die. They have dreams of heaven. Their stories tell me God is there, green meadows, relatives, animals we have loved. This too shall pass - and God will correct it all. Great talking to you Ross.*

I was taken by how deeply she bared her soul. I wrote her an encouraging reply: *"So much depth in your post. Sending a blanket prayer your way."*

The next day I got a reply from her account. It was written by Julia Anne's husband, Scott: *"This is Julia's husband Scott. Julia passed away yesterday in her sleep. She got solace from your words and suggestions to journal and meditate. But this world was too much for her so now she is with Jesus. Continue your work and postings to help others."*

## What's In This For You?

*Emile Griffith and Julia Anne Throckmorton-Miller remind us that many people are fighting a secret war we cannot know. Why not choose to treat everyone as if they are carrying a private burden? Before we speak in public or write words on a page, let's make sure we are exhibiting kindness, caring, empathy, and positivity. Spreading peace is your best weapon against misinterpretation.*

# CHAPTER 12

# Practice Confidence

*By Allison Dalvit*

## Why Read This Story?

*If you are working at a job you despise, it means you quit interviewing too soon. Maybe you took the job because you were desperate for cash. This story will give you three rules for waiting until you land the job that fits.*

Growing up, I never knew I was supposed to pay my dues and work for bad organizations.

That option never occurred to me because I had two loving, encouraging parents.

They taught me no accomplishment was out of reach if (1) I went after the job rather than wait for it to come to me, (2) I had a disciplined work ethic and (3) was tough enough to handle rejection.

That easy? I never questioned it.

Working hard and not "personalizing" rejection led me to become an all-state tennis player, win lead roles in school plays, and even get a casting tryout with TV producer Aaron Spelling's new show titled "Angels '88." By the way, I wasn't impressed with the show and told Mr. Spelling I'd be at Colorado State University if he wanted to find me. (A higher education was more important to me than chasing pretend bad guys.)

As a teenager, I was often told I had an unusually high level of confidence. Hmm, I didn't know confidence was "unusual."

By the summer of 1987, at 17, I was already thinking about finding a job. I didn't know where I wanted to work but I knew I wanted to be financially self-sufficient.

I had a plan to attack any company within a 10-mile radius of my house. Over that summer, I interviewed for over 40 jobs.

I wasn't scared at all.

I got a rush out of it.

Some days I'd have multiple interviews. I got pretty good at answering tough questions. "Can you work weekends and holidays?" "Do you get along well with others?" "What kind of experience do you have?" With that much time in the interview chair, I found that I could take control of the interview and learn about them. I'd ask, "Tell me why I should work here?" "What happens if I have a family emergency?" All of that practice with hiring managers boosted my already high self-confidence. I was offered almost every job I sought. With so many offers, I chose the ones that sounded fun. When I took a job that ultimately wasn't a good fit, I never felt guilty about quitting.

• I worked at the gyro stand for one hour.

Why did I quit? During training, I was warned that previous employees had lost fingers with the extremely sharp knife needed to carve meat off of the rotating meat stick. I loved my pinky finger too much to stay.

- I worked as a Bennigan's restaurant waitress for three days.

Why did I quit? When an overly flirtatious customer asked if I was on the menu and smacked my butt, and management did nothing about it, I left.

- The Senior Housing Center as a nurse assistant for 30 minutes.

Why did I quit? During orientation I was told I would have to change the diapers of seniors. I would have to soap them up in the shower, and get them dressed for the day. My first assignment was to help an elderly man with his dentures. I kept trying to jam his teeth into his mouth and he resisted. Turns out he was saying, "Those aren't my teeth!" I headed for the exit before it was my turn for the diaper assignment.

Call me cocky if you want, but remember, I was a teenager whose parents convinced me my dream job was waiting for me as long as I worked hard and could handle rejection.

I finally found my best fit at BC Surf and Sport. I loved being in a retail store that represented the beach. Since I lived in Colorado, we didn't sell many surfboards, but the vibe was cool and my coworker peeps were 'my kind of people.' I'd work there for the rest of my high school years.

But what would I do after high school?

"Don't wait around for someone to offer you the perfect job," said my folks.

If you want a great job, you have to chase after it with a vengeance. Be more prepared and more experienced than your competition.

Yeah, you've heard that before but where do you get experience if there is no job?

Ah, I was ready for that question.

You have to create experience where none existed before.

While I was working at the surf shop, I already knew I wanted to be a television newscaster. In those days, there were no "communication" classes. How was I supposed to get any experience?

I figured if there were no jobs, I'd invent my own job.

I shot my own cable TV show. I used the family video recorder with me as "the anchor" and I'd include anything that was happening in my high school (Columbine Rebels). Then, I'd send the raw tapes to a local cable channel. I called my show "Rebel Yell" and our local cable station aired the show two times a week.

I was getting experience as a TV anchor and a producer.

I also created my own "lunchtime radio station."

Ok, I'm exaggerating a bit. Actually, the school would let me sit in the lunchroom closet with a microphone connected to a speaker that could be heard throughout the lunch area. I would play my mix tapes and banter to the lunch crowd for that hour every day.

When I wasn't on cable TV or in a lunchroom closet clicking cassettes, my other high school "job" was emcee of the pep rallies. Too much was never enough.

Although I wasn't getting paid, I was getting airtime! I never cared about the money because I believed that every experience in life was preparing me for something else.

In college, I worked (unpaid) for the college radio station (KCSU) as an overnight disc jockey. I was also a member of The Advertising Club, which allowed me to insert myself into local advertising promotions. I did everything I could to get in front of an audience.

It was experience, baby!

By my senior year, I had a full-time radio shift from 6 p.m.-midnight on the "Top 20" station in town. Nobody cared that most of my experience was done for free. My resume was growing and invaluable for snagging me internships at Denver's ABC and NBC affiliates (KUSA and KCNC respectively).

Excessive effort always attracts attention and, eventually, gets rewarded.

My college professor saw my dedication and picked me to represent Colorado State University at the annual NPPA (National Press Photographers Association) conference in Oklahoma. It was there I met top NBC reporter Bob Dotson, whose series, "The American Story," aired on *The Today Show* for 40 years.  Since I have never shied from rejection, I introduced myself to Bob. I couldn't stop talking and asking him questions. He could see I was hungry and hyper…and that his only escape was to teach me, mentor me and train me to become a journalist/reporter.

Did my diligence (some called it an obsession) pay off?

Thanks to the early advice from Mom and Dad, I graduated from college in 3 ½ years and had a real news anchor job before my classmates even ordered their caps and gowns.

What imaginary obstacle is stopping you?

## What's In This For You?

*Don't make your job search about who pays you the most money. Make it about your joy and enthusiasm for doing the work. If you made a mistake, and you hate the job so much you want to quit, then quit. Don't settle for a job that makes you want to call in sick.*

# CHAPTER 13

# Forget Defeat

*By Ross Shafer*

## Why Read This Story?

*We've studied why some people succeed and why others fail. Turns out success in life is about having the resilience to fight another day. You don't need a 5-step formula. You only need to repeat TWO profound words in order to survive your flubs and remain confident about your destination.*

In first and second grades I attended an inner-city elementary school. The city was Portland, Oregon. It was a rugged timber town in those days. My mom made me go to school with Band-Aids in my pockets because she knew the kids in my neighborhood were tough, or at least trying to prove they were.

Several times, older boys would push me down the long slide or yank me off the monkey bars. My hands would tear open on the metal seams and…sometimes I'd want to cry. I never did. Even if my hands were wounded and bleeding, I'd look at my attacker and say, "So what, Monkey Butt! That didn't hurt." Then, I'd lick the blood and spit it back at him.

FYI: Spit blood at a second grader and they think you're too crazy to fight.

I'd go home and my mom would refill my pockets with Band-Aids.

I don't remember where I first heard the phrase, "So what, Monkey Butt?!" but I assumed it was just sassy playground slang.

In high school I ran across "So what?!" in the Oxford Dictionary, which officially defined those words to mean, "I don't care," "It's not a big deal," "Whatever happened doesn't matter to me." I'd made those words fit in second grade and didn't even know it.

By the time I got to college, I resolved that "So what?" would be the most memorable (and motivational) words I would ever hear.

By the end of this story, you'll never forget the words "So what?!" either.

In college, I played linebacker for the University of Puget Sound in Tacoma, Washington. We were coached by this six foot five inch, 260-pound beast of a man named Paul Wallrof. We called him Big Wally.

Big Wally had been a star offensive tackle at the University of Washington in Seattle and his enthusiasm for the game caused him to reject any other sensible job. He was aggressive and excitable. Sometimes to the point of using words that made no sense like, "I'm about to buy you a ticket to a place I've never been." But then again, what 20-year-old questions a big, loud, spit-when-he-talks coach?

When Wally was fired up, his voice could be heard 300 miles away in Idaho. Big Wally was tough. He was demanding. He was relentless. And, we all loved him. He was our champion. He took time to make you a better ballplayer.

And when he did get the words right, you would never forget it.

When the other team scored a touchdown, Big Wally would bellow, "SO WHAT?!"

When the other team intercepted a pass, he'd scream, "SO WHAT?!"

If your hands slipped a tackle and the other team got a first down, Wally would run over to you, get an inch from your grill and boom, "SO WHAT?!"

"So what" were the most encouraging words a ball player could ever hear because Big Wally wasn't roaring to belittle us. He wasn't trying to shame us into playing better. "So what?!" was his rallying cry for us NOT to dwell on our mistakes. He wanted us to dismiss our errors and turn our focus to the next play.

I've played for coaches who thought they could motivate an athlete by demeaning them. "I've never seen anyone so pathetic," "Stop tackling like a little baby," and "You aren't good enough to wear that uniform." Public shaming (amongst your peers) is a stupid technique. It fosters resentment. I never wanted to play for, or work for, a jerk who got off on pulling rank.

Big Wally's words, "So what?!" didn't shame anyone or single us out. His words were directed to all of us…because after all, we were a team.

"So what?!" became so infamous that we parroted him off the field. If we were out at a bar and somebody broke a beer mug, all of us would chant, "So what?!" If one of the players was almost in tears over a breakup we'd yell, "So what?!"

Big Wally gave us a perspective that worked for almost everything.

I want "So what?!" to be as relevant to your life as it was for the hundreds of football players Big Wally coached.

If you don't close a sale you thought was a sure thing, tell yourself, "So what?!" and move onto the next lead.

If you miss a customer meeting because you got distracted and marked 6 p.m. instead of 6 a.m., that's a "So what?!" moment.

How about when one of your coworkers blows an assignment that you had to jump in and clean up? Think how motivating it would be if you approached that person and said, "You didn't do this on purpose. So what?! I'll help you with the next one."

None of our careers are judged by a single blunder. Nobody likes to screw up, but you can always diffuse an awkward situation with "So what?!"  By not making a big deal out of failure, you are showing others that redemption is possible.

In fact, Big Wally used to say, "If you're not making mistakes, you're not trying."

Basketball legend Michael Jordan was asked, "After missing three shots in a row, are you nervous you might miss the next three too?" Jordan said, "I am never nervous about a shot I haven't taken yet." Jordan doesn't let his past missteps affect his future.

You want to know the lasting power of "SO WHAT?"

Thirty-years after we played football at UPS, about 60 of us organized a football reunion to celebrate Coach Wallrof's 80th birthday. All these decades later, the young men who heard him holler "SO WHAT?!" had been transformed. Everyone I talked to had become resilient, successful men who never forgot the two simple words that have shaped our personal and professional lives.

Thanks, Coach.

## What's In This For You?

*The lesson here is to stop deliberating about your past failures. We tend to look back to see how badly we disappointed the people we love. But what if the people we care about treated us with a "So what" attitude and remained hopeful for better results? Most people feel that way. You see flaws in yourself that others don't. Stop it.*

*Paul Wallrof kept all of us
from being easily rattled
by a bad play.*

# CHAPTER 14

# Recognize You

*By Allison Dalvit*

## Why Read This Story?

*You probably don't see yourself as the world sees you. Take, Leonardo Di Vinci's* Mona Lisa. *For over 500 years scholars have been speculating about the state of Mona's mood. (By the way, she was a real model.) If she were alive today, would Mona enlighten us with the real meaning of her half smile? This story will change your mind about how you are seen by the world.*

My mother taught me to appreciate fine art so deeply that certain paintings overtake my emotions. I can stare at them for hours.

Mom is an artist who knows the difference between a heavy parallel brush stroke and a shadowy one. She scrimped and saved to buy a real Picasso. She also purchased an Erte, a Michael Parks, a Salvador Dali, and several sexy oil paintings from the Mexican realist Juan Medina. Born in Mexico City in 1950, Medina was exposed to cultural diversity. His work is *suis generis* ("one of a kind") because it merges ancient Indian and Spanish cultures. He later relocated to Paris, France, to be inspired by art history and devote himself to painting. Juan Medina might not be as well-known as Dali or Picasso, but his art has hung in the Louvre Museum in Paris, France.

While Picasso's art came to life as Cubism and collage, Medina's oil paintings were inspired by the stories he heard from his subjects. Every brush stroke was in service of sharing these stories.

I know this because I met Juan and his wife Griselda Medina.

They flew into Louisiana from Paris to attend a New Orleans art exhibit held in their honor. My mother owned many of his paintings and we couldn't wait to meet them. Juan was very quiet but quite smiley. (I would be smiley too if my paintings brought in $20,000 each.)

Juan was very excited to finally visit Louisiana. In 1993, Bryant Allen, owner of Bryant Art Galleries saw an image by Juan Medina in *ARTNews* magazine. Bryant flew to Cuernavaca, Mexico, to meet the artist. He was so taken with Juan's art, he flew home with several paintings and sold them right away.

At the art exhibit, held in New Orleans, Louisiana, the Medinas showed up prim, proper, and polite. Never shy, my mother and I introduced ourselves. After our short conversation with them, I sensed they yearned to soak up the infamous New Orleans lore. They knew about the Mardi Gras celebrations, the craziness, and the legends. They beamed when I offered to parade them around town after the art show.

We started at the World Trade Center, at the Top of the Mart rooftop club, where we danced on the rotating floor beneath our feet. The walls were made of glass, so you got a breathtaking 360-degree view of New Orleans. We drank plenty of Juan's favorite tequila (it may have been the French brand, El Mayor). After four or five shots, who cares? A Big Easy friendship was born.

We ended the night at about 4 a.m. We hugged. We exchanged contact information. We promised to stay in touch; even though we both knew that probably wouldn't happen.

Still, a glorious once-in-a-lifetime night.

You can imagine my surprise when I got an email from Juan after he and Griselda returned to Paris. I was suddenly a pen pal with a famous artist and his wife!

I was even more stunned when Juan and Griselda invited me to visit Paris so they could show me around their town. The invitation to see Paris, alongside a world-renowned artist, blew my freaking mind!

But I couldn't do it.

As exhilarated as I was by their offer, I was embarrassed to tell them, *"I am so sorry, Mr. Medina…I am afraid to fly."*

Juan wouldn't let me slide on my "no fly zone" excuse. He started quizzing me about my trepidations. He wanted to know the history. The anxiety. The irrationality. He wanted to peel the onion, layer-by-layer, to get at the core of my fears.

Then, the bombshell I didn't see coming.

He wanted to paint my story, with me as the model!

Uh, I knew his work. Many of his paintings were of beautiful, very nude, women. I respectfully declined.

If you think this sounds like the perfect scheme of a creep to get women naked, you'd be wrong.

I soon learned that posing nude in person didn't matter.

He was after my story. For months, via email, he would ask

me questions to better understand my flight terrors. He wanted the backstory, a detailed depiction for his art.

Paint me he did.

A few months later, *Afraid of Flying* hit the gallery.

The canvas held the image of a young brunette woman (dare I say a dead ringer for me) with dark blue wings, perched on a white pillar, looking through a beautiful stained-glass window. The scene, from the inside, was dark—lots of cold concrete walls as if to encage her. Outside, there was light and beauty. The image was so powerful, yet so tragic. She couldn't move from her perch—even though freedom lay inches away.

Juan's art brought tears to my eyes.

*Afraid of Flying* represented everything that had held me down—unhealthy relationships, toxic people, moral dilemmas, and sticky situations. All of the above contributed to my fear of flying. His message was therapy for me. Juan Medina only knew me from an art party, a cocktail lounge, and our emails. Yet, as an artist trained to express truth, he saw everything I couldn't see. He captured me in an unspoken expression—my proximity to my own freedom. Why couldn't I just fly? Juan wrote to me with this explanation: *"There are so many ways of being afraid to fly. Wings are a symbol of the freedom of doing it. Furthermore, of the possibility of doing it. But we have been SO told that we mustn't - that we shouldn't - even from a privileged spot and having all means - that we don't know we can fly. We would have to free our mind and believe we can do it. Fear will disappear as soon as we take off."*

I was suddenly determined to fly free of my fears.

Thanks to Juan Medina, I fly. I became unwilling to engage in toxic friendships. I am no longer hostage to the unhealthy marriages I left behind. I don't suffer fools and liars. I never stay too long in a dead-end job. I run from meaningless situations.

Okay, and I can actually get on airplanes, too.

Mystical side note? I have a giclée fine art print of *Afraid of Flying* hanging in my home. Over time, the ink used for the dark blue wings has all but faded completely away. Ironically, the wings faded just about the time I flew from the perch.

## What's In This For You?

*We don't know each other yet, but I can predict you do not completely see yourself as the world sees you. Maybe you need someone you trust to hold your persona up to a mirror like Juan Medina did for me? The result profoundly changed my life. If you don't know how you project yourself, it will make getting to know someone an exercise of fraud.*

*What you see here is the painting he did of me; even though I never modeled for him.*

*My mother and I met Juan Medina and his lovely wife Griselda in New Orleans at a gallery showing of his beautiful work. We became fast friends and partied like rock stars.*

# CHAPTER 15

# Intimidate Me

*By Ross Shafer*

## Why Read This Story?

*If you suffer from being intimidated to talk to people because you consider them superior to you, this story is for you.*

Why do certain people intimidate you?

- Is it because these people make more money?
- Do these people appear to have more influence?
- Have they achieved a higher rank or social status?

The quick answer is because you don't believe they see you as an equal.

Ergo, the antidote for being less awed is to become an equal.

Trust me, at some point your imaginary "idols" felt exactly how you're feeling right now.

I have three paths for you to become less intimidated.

## Be Interested in Other People

Gregory Peck intimidated me. His voice. His stature. His charisma.

As a network talk show host, I had talked to celebrities every night.

Gregory Peck was different. I'd seen the classic movie *To Kill a Mockingbird* about a thousand times so when I saw Mr. Peck in person, behind the stage curtain, I was so enamored I could barely raise my arm for a handshake.

Then, I noticed he was shuffling his feet and pulling at his collar. He was a wreck. I asked, "Are you ok? Do you need some water?" Peck said, "I watch you every night and I'm afraid I'm going to screw up your show. I'm not good without a script. What could I possibly say of any interest? I haven't made a good movie in ten years." I said, "I was just going to ask you some questions about what you do for fun when you're not working." (At this point, I thought he might bolt.) "I've got an idea. Let's rehearse it right here." I found when I asked genuine questions that were all about his personal life (not movies), and I responded with a smile, quickly asking a follow up question about him, something unexpected happened.

Mr. Peck calmed down.

I didn't have to prove I was worthy to chat with Gregory Peck because he was more intimidated by going on a national television show with ME. I released him from judging his own performance as a human being.

## Fake Some Confidence

This sounds like a trick but it's not.

You're a smart person who knows how to do your job. It's likely that nobody knows how to do your job as well as you can.

Start practicing having more confidence in your work (not bragging…just get better at explaining your processes).

Having confidence in your specialty will win the respect of a boss, a manager, or for that matter, any stakeholder in your company. You just have to be willing to talk about what you do…with a strong voice, eye contact, and assuredness. When a higher-up asks you, "How's it going?" be clear-minded. Explain what matters to them and show some enthusiasm. What matters? Results!

I cannot emphasize the word enthusiasm enough because enthusiasm is an indicator that you have a pulse!

You might even have a personality!

You aren't quiet and boring anymore!

You are starting to sound interesting!

The people who used to intimidate you now think there is value in talking to you!

Practice talking about results and "amping up" your enthusiasm until it starts to feel natural to you. Then, wait for your opportunity to break out of your intimidated shell.

## Make Your Boss Look Good

Let's say you work for a boss who thinks he/she knows it all. You try to share your groundbreaking ideas to make the company better and you're met with insolence, "That's a really dumb idea. We're going to do it my way."

It's wrong but it's still intimidating.

A prick like that just signaled you aren't a peer. You're a stupid underling. Sadly, you might never bring up another idea again.

You can become a peer if you know what every boss wants.

Senior leaders will respect you if (1) you show them how to make more money or (2) show them how to save more money.

In the opening example, let's revisit why you didn't hit peer status.

Why did the boss prefer his/her idea over yours?

Were you prepared enough to have that conversation?

Was your idea too vague—no specifics?

Did you present A, B and C options?

Did you freeze up when the boss brought up objections?

Ah…then you failed at your goals to make the boss look good.

Every boss (even a prick) will listen to a clever idea for growing revenue. If you can put together a viable step-by-step plan, you will stand out from coworkers who just want to show up, punch a clock, and go home.

Furthermore, if you can provide an endless stream of well-organized ideas, you become invaluable. You will elevate yourself to peer status.

## I've Saved the Best for Last…

All three techniques have one thing in common--they are all stitched together by the 'other-focused' thread.

You will establish instant rapport if you focus on what is most important to them.

Ask about their animals. Ask about their awards. As for their advice. Ask about a mutual hobby. Ask what keeps them up at night. Premeditate a list of questions you think people would like to answer about themselves. Then, rehearse those questions so they dance off your tongue easily.

When you showed confidence in doing your job, you made your boss feel smart for hiring you.

When you impressed the boss with your money-making (or money-saving) ideas, you gave him/her the prospect of looking smart to his or her boss.

When I coaxed Gregory Peck to rehearse answers about his off-camera life (pets, children, hobbies,) he could answer comfortably—and without fear—because he knew what was coming.

Being 'other focused' is the most powerful skill you can hone. Here's why.

We live in a social media-obsessed society where Facebook, Instagram, Twitter, and Snapchat are populated by self-absorbed people who post every tedious detail of their lives. (Pics of your leftover lunch? Really?) Most posts reveal people who are in desperate need of attention and validation.

When you show interest in other people, you are celebrating them. You are validating them. Most people would love to talk to you...*about themselves.* They trust you because their brains register that you just "liked" them.

You can become anyone's peer if you make every conversation about the other person.

## What's In This For You?

*It's natural to be intimidated by people you think are smarter, wiser, and more experienced. Please relax! You will find yourself in rare company if you realize the people you admire all started at the bottom and felt the same intimidation when they were in your shoes.*

*A comedy concert celebrating comedian Mort Sahl's 80th birthday. TOP ROW DOWN: Kevin Nealon, Richard Lewis, Jay Leno, Norm Crosby, Hugh Hefner, Me, Drew Carey, Albert Brooks, Shelley Berman, Jonathan Winters, George Carlin, Mort Sahl, Harry Shearer.*

*The nicest famous man in the world, Henry Winkler (The Fonz). My lifelong pal Bill Nye (The Science Guy). Forced to defend myself against Heavyweight Champ, George Foreman.*

# CHAPTER 16

# Question Reality

*By Allison Dalvit*

## Why Read This Story?

*Have you ever been shocked by someone who appears to be a benevolent person in public, yet becomes quite unsavory behind closed doors? How is that possible? There is a clue in this story.*

Warning: Never piss off Santa Claus.

He might leave behind more than a lump of coal.

I was working on a holiday show for the Food Network and I needed to cast an authentic-looking Santa Claus. I needed my Santa to open our show with a jolly, "HO, HO, HO," and walk across the stage dressed in full Santa regalia.

The supervising producer requested I find a Santa with a real beard…not a costume beard.  I was surprised to learn that "Real Bearded Santas" were listed all over the internet.

In a matter of minutes, I was auditioning a dozen cheery Santas. I say "cheery" because these guys took this job seriously. They become Santa Claus in looks, voice, full costume, and the requisite "Ho-Ho-Ho" joviality.

They were all so good, I felt confident I could pull a name out of a hat and cast my perfect Santa.

That's precisely what I did.

Santa #7 got the gig.

I thanked all of the other Santa applicants and wished them a "Merry Christmas." Lots of fun. No hard feelings. Actors are used to going from one audition to the next.

After the auditions, we all went back to our respective desks to plot out the rest of the show. About a half hour later, our front desk receptionist called me, "Allison, Santa is here to see you." I assumed our guy wanted more information about the shoot. When I saw him, he was dressed in a red sweatshirt and blue jeans. He still looked exactly like Santa Claus, but I suspected this was not my Santa.

The giveaway was sensing this Santa was on the verge of… furious.

He was cradling a rolled-up newspaper in his left arm, glaring at me, "Are you Allison? The gal casting Santa for the Food Network?" I smiled and said I was. He moved toward me, "Why didn't you pick me?! Don't you think I look like Santa Claus?"

In a nano-second I knew whatever I said next wouldn't be good enough.

In my head, I knew he looked exactly like Santa. But I'd rejected this guy. I didn't mean to insult anyone. I assumed men who dressed up like Santa for TV auditions were just having fun with this. I've cast a lot of actors and they usually expect they may only get 10% of their auditions anyway.

At this moment, my previous rationale was useless.

I had an angry Santa Claus towering over me with a rolled-up newspaper.

Imagine the paradox.

I love everything about Santa Claus. I never thought Santa could be dangerous—until right then.

I scanned his newspaper, predicting a hidden weapon.

Was he hiding a knife? A gun? Anthrax powder?

My fight or flight response was preparing me to cover my face or run for cover.

Lifting his right arm shoulder-high Santa's clone threw the rolled-up newspaper at my feet and ran for the door.

We all freaked!

Was it a bomb? Toxic warfare?

Luckily, no.

Careful examination revealed the rolled-up newspaper was filled with fresh dog poop.

We called security.

I logged into my computer to identify which of the 12 Santa actors had just scared the hell out of us. I couldn't differentiate a singular suspect.

As it turns out, "Santa" is an excellent disguise.

Even if I had demanded a police lineup, one pudgy, white-bearded Santa Claus looks like every other pudgy, white-bearded Santa Claus. What if I had picked the wrong man out of the lineup? There is no way I could send an innocent Santa to the hoosegow.

All we could do was beef up security.

Throughout the entire shoot, my colleagues escorted me to and from my car.

The whole episode was a huge lesson in pre-judgment.

I had made two false assumptions.

First: I assumed that just because an actor dresses up like Santa Claus does not mean he absorbs the personality of the costume. I fell for the obvious misdirection.

Second: Rejection is a bitch, even for Santa Claus.

I saw a dozen Santas and assumed they were an interchangeable commodity.

As human beings, none of us are interchangeable. We all believe we deserve to be judged independently.

Maybe, I should have been more appreciative of each actor in that group. Maybe I should have explained why I chose one Santa over another. I wonder if I should have told them all how difficult a decision this was "…because you are all so convincing."

Regardless, I have never been that generic in my casting choices since.

I'll tell you one thing. I'll never look at a mall Santa or a bell ringer the same way…not since one Santa gifted me with something much worse than a lump of coal.

## What's In This For You?

*It's hard to get a bead on a person's unvarnished character solely based upon their outward appearance and style. You already know that actions speak louder than words. Only judge a person's character when their actions don't sync up with their public "presentation."*

# CHAPTER 17

# Notice Deceit

*By Ross Shafer*

## Why Read This Story?

*As much as we want to see the best in people, many will disappoint you. The hurt is much worse when the betrayal comes from someone you wholly trust. This story will help you discern poor character in such people...before it's too late.*

My best male friend in the world hurt me so badly I lost my only source of family income—as well as our five-year friendship.

I never saw it coming. It destroyed my faith in people for a long time.

I hope a betrayal like this doesn't befall you, but we can't possibly know what lurks in the hearts and minds of the people closest to us...or can we?

I first met Mark Sacks when I was a freshman in college.

Football season was over, and damn, I needed money to fuel my VW Bug so I could go on dates. I applied for a salesman job at an upscale clothing store called The Haberdash. While I didn't have any sales experience, I had worked at an Arco gas station and won the "Friendliest Employee" award the previous summer. Hey, I thought that item on my resume would land any job. It got a laugh out of the store manager, Mark Sacks, who said, "Let's see how friendly you are after I train you."

Mark was tall and slender, which made everything he wore look like he'd just stepped out of a Nordstrom catalog. His blond mane flowed with his balanced gait. He smoked thin brown cigarettes. Overall, his demeanor was smooth, funny, and his sales skills were epic. Mark treated every customer as if he were dressing a king; lifting the jacket so it would easily glide over the man's shoulders. It was artful. I believed he could sell anything.

Mark taught me how to talk to wealthy customers, how to match complex neckties with suits, how to make people feel good about my suggestions and how to upsell an extra pair of slacks with every sport coat. I didn't have Mark's grace but I learned how to sell.

After work, we became best pals.

When the store closed, we would frequent a local sports bar. That's where I learned Mark was a skillful pool shark. If I thought he was smooth on the sales floor, I was astonished by his ability to find suckers. He'd challenge someone to a game and then play badly, losing maybe a hundred bucks or more. He was always dressed well so his opponents would figure this guy had money to burn.

When the bets got over $300 a game, Mark would start sinking every shot and walk away with all of the other guy's money. He was an excellent actor, pretending he just got lucky. We'd have a big laugh in the parking lot and he'd say, "Don't tell Cindy (his wife). She'd just want to spend it on groceries or drapes."

I worked at The Haberdash for about 18 months until I got a football scholarship to a four-year college, 300 miles away.

Fast forward two years.

I was 22 when I graduated from college and took a job as a comptroller for a chain of Big and Tall clothing stores.

I'd stayed in touch with my buddy Mark, and at one point, he asked me if I could put in a word with the hiring manager at my new company.

This was a no-brainer. We'd die to have someone with Mark's skills.

I got him a job at our flagship store, and I found an apartment for him and Cindy, just a block from my own apartment.

Having my friend in the company building was so much fun!

We would meet up after hours for beers. Most days, we'd carpool to and from work. I was also married and the four of us got together at least four nights a week for dinner and a bottle of Cold Duck or Blue Nun.

It was like we had gotten the band back together.

The only hiccups were when Mark's wife, Cindy, would call to ask when he'd be home. She was pregnant with their first child. If he had a billiards dolt on the hook, he'd have me call Cindy and tell her he was stuck with inventory counts—or staying late with our best customer. Yeah, I was his accomplice, but Mark told me he was saving his pool winnings to surprise his wife with a house. I thought that was pretty cool, and besides, I'd never had this much fun with any other coworker.

Mark was my #1 confidant as well.

He was ten years older and wiser—and because he had taught me the finer points of the sales trade, I deferred to his savvy.

One Sunday night, after I'd burned an eight-pack of wieners on the BBQ grill, Mark and I shuffled off to Kentucky Fried Chicken so our wives wouldn't think we were losers.

In the car, I asked his advice about an offer I'd gotten to join an advertising agency. Mark encouraged me to take the job, "That's why you went to college. You'll make a lot more money and you'll get out of this dead-end retail clothing bullshit."

My buddy made sense, but I was still on the fence about changing jobs. My wife was pregnant and I had to be a financially responsible husband and father.

The following Monday morning I got a phone call from the Big and Tall company president.

"I need you in my office right away."

He never called me into his office unless we were closing one of the stores, so I was prepared to review the current leases.

I walked into his office and could tell he was steamed.

"I'm letting you go, Ross…today."

I was flat-footed, "Uh…what?"

"I know you're leaving us for another job. I wish you would have come to me. Mark Sacks is going to take your job."

I'd just been rear-ended by my best friend.

What the hell?! I got him this job. I found a place for him to live. Our families did everything together. I admired him as a friend and mentor. This was impossible, yet undeniably true.

I couldn't wait to track him down and threaten his life.

I found Mark in the shipping center, bragging to the

warehouse manager about "the changes he wants to make when Ross was gone." He didn't see me behind him. I spun him around and grabbed him by his perfectly pressed wide lapel suit and lifted him up—pinning him against the iron beams that separated the pallets (I was a taut 224 pounds from 14 years of football). "I want you to remember this moment. If I ever see you again, I'm going to break every fucking bone in your body!" I threw him down on the cement floor. "Tell me you understand that." I stood hard on his ankle; which was clad in a fashionable half-boot. I twisted my foot on his ankle like I was crushing a cigarette on concrete. Then, I walked away.

I never saw Mark again. Two days later, I saw a moving truck outside his apartment.

I started this story by saying, "I never saw it coming."

I chose to ignore the red flags. These flags were waving all the years that I knew him.

Mark took joy in screwing innocent people out of money as a pool shark.

Mark kept his "billiard winnings" a secret from his wife.

I thought back to the times Mark rendered false stories to customers just to persuade them into spending more money.

I thought about the times Mark asked me to lie to Cindy about his whereabouts. Cindy just wanted an approximate ETA so she could keep his dinner warm.

Later, I heard from a mutual friend that Mark had been a serial cheater and left his wife soon after their daughter was born.

Fifteen years went by before I heard Mark had died from lung cancer. I guess those long thin brown cigarettes caught up to him. Being well dressed and smooth wasn't enough to keep him alive.

I knew this guy was a rat, yet I was so eager to have a fun friend to play with, I overlooked his character and became a pawn in his degenerate motives.

I misjudged him but it's also an unforgivable sin to leverage my insider information to steal my job and bias my soul.

## What's In This For You?

*If you pay attention, character flaws are obvious. Trust the "red flags" of the people you call your friends. If you have a friend whose decisions go against your morality or your values, it's time to distance yourself. Here is a quick test—if your bestie gossips about your mutual friends when they are not around, you should assume you will be "thrown under the bus" when you aren't in the room.*

# CHAPTER 18

# Prevent Regrets

*By Allison Dalvit & Ross Shafer*

## Why Read This Story?

*This is a story about making an impossible decision with your partner. The resolution of a potentially life-threatening situation requires empathy, respect, cooperation, and a sense of a dual mission. Tissue anyone?*

ALLISON: Ross told me his 92-year-old mother was suffering from congestive heart failure, causing her lungs to fill with fluid. She had been in her assisted living center for over two years and was going downhill fast. She was no longer eating or drinking.

ROSS: Under normal circumstances, I would've hopped on a direct flight to Ashland, Oregon, and rushed to be at Mom's side. But because of the Covid-19 pandemic, I couldn't legally get on a plane. Worse, even if I could get to her in time, I wouldn't be allowed to go inside her building. The risks of infection were too high for the elderly.

ALLISON: During our evening call, I heard the frustration and pain in his voice. Ross felt helpless and trapped. It was crushing him that he would never be able to say goodbye to his mother or see her beautiful smile again. She didn't know how to do a FaceTime call. This was the woman he most admired. She nurtured him. She loved him. She was his lifelong champion.

ROSS: I talked to my mother on my cell phone and she understood the circumstances, "I will be fine, Ross. I'm exactly where I need to be and I love you wherever you are, honey." It was killing me. My brother Scott and his wife Rowena assured me Mom was at peace and not to worry.

ALLISON: We were in the first wave of the pandemic, and even if Ross drove his car from Denver, Colorado, to Ashland, Oregon, each of the five contiguous states were in varying degrees of lockdown. Some were barely lifting the stay-at-home orders, one by one, depending upon their governor's comfort level.

ROSS: I was tormented that the five-state drive was such a long haul and there was no guarantee my mother would even be alive when we got there.

ALLISON: I told Ross, "What do you need? No, what do you want? It is time to think about what YOU need right now. If you must see your mother before she passes, then let's figure a way to do this together."

ROSS: I was shocked! Even dumbfounded that Allison proposed this. I am not a person who likes to inconvenience anybody, at any time. Plus, she and I had only been dating a couple of months, and in ten million years I couldn't have imagined Ali would offer to accompany me on this long, potentially danger-ous trip—just so I could give my mom one final wave goodbye. I told Allison I wanted to think about it overnight. (To this day I cannot tell you why I needed "to sleep on it.")

ALLISON: About 7 a.m. the next morning, my phone buzzed. Ross said, "Let's do it!" He concluded he truly needed to see his mom one last time. If there was even a slim chance we'd succeed, it would be something he would cherish for the rest of his life. He was walking the walk...not just talking the talk.

ROSS: Allison convinced me that if you have even the slightest chance to be with the ones you love in their last moments, you must not waste another minute. She made it clear, "Let's keep this trip open-ended. We don't have to be back at any certain time." Seriously, who do you know who is that selfless?

ALLISON: Within two hours, I threw everything I owned in a suitcase. I had no clue how long we would be gone. Would we stay a week? A month? What weather conditions would we experience? I packed all kinds of clothes and filled a cooler with all of the snacks and drinks I could rummage.

ROSS: By noon, Allison, my 14-year-old daughter Lauren, and I were on I-70 Highway heading west, in the middle of a pandemic, sprinting from Colorado to Oregon (with routes through Utah, Nevada, and California). One way it was 22 hours—1,235 miles.

ALLISON: We didn't know if gas stations would be open. What about hotels? Would we be able to find a restroom? We really had no idea about any of it. I packed a roll of toilet paper and hand wipes in case we ran into trouble.

ROSS: THANK GOD we didn't need to find a tree along the way! Each town was a ghost town. Some restrooms were closed. Good thing Allison brought snacks and drinks because food was scarce. The lockdowns kept the highways empty. It was almost like, as we were driving, each state was slowly opening as we pulled in. It was that surreal.

ALLISON: If you only know a person for a couple of months, a trip like this could be a deal breaker for a new couple. We kind of knew that going in. But, this wasn't a vacation. We were on a mission of seeking life. We held hands, played music, shared stories, and encouraged each other during this hellacious journey. Not a single disagreement or annoyance surfaced.

ROSS: I would check in with my brother from time to time and he wasn't hopeful we'd make it. According to Mom's nurses, she was fading fast. So, we pushed hard, with limited stops and untenable weather. Road conditions and construction conditions slowed us down. Somehow we kept pressing.

ALLISON: I knew how emotional this was for Ross. Almost anticipating the worst, I did everything I could to make this a positive experience for him. But I won't lie. It was scary. One stretch of our journey was in the middle of nowhere. Barren landscape. Not even a gas station. We drove for hours with no cell phone signal—no sign of life. In my mind, this was a "love wins" race to the finish line.

ROSS: After a dozen hours or so, we pulled into a hotel in Salt Lake City. All of us were exhausted from the pressure of the circumstances. Lauren and I stayed in one room while Ali had the room next door. I went over to thank her for all of this. She surprised me with a bottle of wine, cheese, and crackers. I have never experienced such generosity and thoughtfulness. What an amazing person to give up her life for an unknown period of time—to spearhead something so important to myself and my daughter.

ALLISON: We got an early start the next day and twelve hours later we wheeled into the quaint town of Ashland, Oregon. We drove straight to the nursing home. Did we make it in time?

ROSS: My heart was pounding outside of my chest. We'd made it to Mom's facility but with the coronavirus being such a deadly threat for seniors, we knew we would not be allowed inside her building. So, I knocked on the outside of Mom's bedroom window. No answer. We couldn't see inside—no lights—but I kept knocking.

ALLISON: We were all so anxious. She was either asleep—or we were too late. Suddenly his mom appeared, framed by her bedroom window. Her room was dark, but when she clicked on the small table lamp beside her, she looked like an angel.

ROSS: I called her room phone. We were actually able to speak to each other! I couldn't believe we made it! Mom has always had such an incredible sense of humor and she was in full voice now! "Hiiiii Ross! Hiii Lolo!" I could barely see out of my wet eyes. I got to say everything I ever needed to say to her and my heart was brimming with love from the woman who raised me, taught me, encouraged me, and loved me for six decades. Of course, I would have loved to hug her but, for a pandemic, I was so satisfied for this moment. God bless Allison Dalvit for making this happen.

ALLISON: The next day, Ross's mother requested hospice care, "I'm on my way out and I'm ready." It was almost as if she was waiting to see her oldest son before she made this final move of acceptance.

ROSS: My brother Scott and I coordinated hospice care per her doctor's recommendation. And surprisingly, when hospice got involved, the senior center loosened the rules on family visitors! Lauren and I were allowed to get into Mom's room (wearing masks and gloves). We could hug her, sit on her bed with her, and laugh with her. I even asked her on video, "Mom, give some 'Grandma the Great' advice to your grandchildren and great grandchildren." Our long sojourn evaporated and was replaced with the warm feeling of doing the right, best thing.

ALLISON: After a two-day visit, we felt we had to go back home. We were hearing about more state-by-state pandemic shutdowns and we were pushing our own luck. We didn't want to catch the coronavirus so far from home. The drive back to Colorado was far less stressful. Ross smiled constantly. He replayed every moment of his visit for most of the long drive home. He even shared the story during a spam call with a random cable TV provider.

ROSS: Once the hospice team lifted the visitation restrictions, my two grown sons, Adam and Ryan, drove down from Seattle to see their grandmother in person. At first, she didn't recognize them with their full beards, so they both shaved their faces clean! My younger brother, Clell, who was distraught over not being able to see mom, was finally able to hug her and deliver his homemade treats.

Mom transitioned peacefully with my brother, Scott, by her side. As she took her last breath, Scott was playing the song, *Hallelujah* by K.D. Lang, Mom's favorite song. We all knew the next leg of her journey would be to reunite with our father, her husband of 53 years.

Was her remaining time revitalized by the avalanche of family visits, well-wishers and hugs?

No question. Love wins.

## What's In This For You?

*Some of life's petrifying conundrums can yield the most character-building memories. As you calculate the threat of danger vs. the potential for the best out-come, consider how your lack of action will play into the weight of your regret. If you still can't decide, just start your car's engine and go.*

*Due to Covid, my daughter Lauren and I were only allowed to see my mom through the bedroom window of her assisted living facility. She appeared like an angel in full possession of her love for others and her indefatigable sense of humor.*

*My sons Ryan and Adam drove down from Bellevue, WA and shaved their full beards so Grandma would recognize them.*

*This is the last time I saw my mother. I will always remember her cracking jokes, playing, laughing, and loving every minute of her precious life.*

# CHAPTER 19

# Rewrite Legacy

*By Ross Shafer*

## Why Read This Story?

*You are going to die. What kind of legacy will you leave? I hope this story will motivate you to change your future, while you still can.*

You still have time to rewrite your tombstone.

Some of you might need to.

I've known a lot of dead people who made an impression. (See chapter 7.)

A few of the rich ones wanted to be memorialized by stamping their name on a hospital wing. Others wanted a theatre dedicated by them. Still others thought it best for people to see their moniker embossed in iron as they entered a stadium.

Is that the purpose of legacy? Or, is it merely trying to finance immortality?

My friend Don Johnson (not the actor) is a popular officiant at funerals. He's a legacy expert.

Strangers hire Don because he's an articulate and funny person who has a way of reflecting well on loved ones. He's so convincing that guests believe Don is the secret best friend nobody knew existed.

I hope you get a chance to attend one of Don's funny funerals. He celebrates the best in people by gently shedding light on their fun quirks. In addition to his memorable eulogies, as a pastor, Don has also baptized hundreds of babies and conducted countless marriages. He tells me, "My job is to hatch, match, and dispatch the best people in the world."

One day, over lunch, I was curious, "Donny, people think you know a side of the dearly departed that even they didn't know. Does anybody ever quiz you for more information?" Don threw his head back, "Yeah, without exception, some guy will come up to me after the service and whisper, 'How much did he leave?' I tell him, 'All of it!'"

In Don's words, "The irony is, money has no value when used as the currency of legacy. The only meaningful 'score card' in life is if you made people feel loved while you were here."

According to Don, making people feel loved isn't always an easy task.

Like you, I had two parents.

I didn't give their legacy much thought until after they were gone. So, I used Don's insight to score my parents.

Until I was about 35, my father and I had a contentious relationship. He didn't pay much attention to me. His work caused him to travel every week. At 13, Dad told me I was "the man of the house." I had the responsibility but none of the authority. When Dad was home, he spent most of his time at the small airport in our town, where he worked on his pride a joy, a one-passenger

Pitts Special biplane. During those years, I really didn't know him.

As long as I can remember, he wanted me to be a lawyer. This was a conflict.

I wanted to be an entertainer.

Hence, I never felt I measured up to what he expected of me.

When he died, all of us were ringed around his hospital bed for his last breath. I hate to admit that I didn't cry for at least a year.

It was at that time, his legacy started showing up.

I began to meet people who told me stories about my father.

*"Christmas decorations were a big deal in our neighborhood. We had a contest every year. One year I broke my leg and couldn't climb the ladder and your dad put up a thousand or more lights for us. I tried to pay him but all he wanted was a little eggnog."*

*"I owe a lot to your father. I lost my job in the ice storm of '67 and couldn't afford fuel oil for our boiler (house furnace). He showed up every week and refilled our tank for free. We'd have frozen to death if not for him."*

*"Your daddio always kept my lawn mower and chain saw running. He knew I wasn't mechanical so once a year he would come over with his tools and ask, 'What's broken?' I'd get a cold beer and Charlie would supply the dirty joke. Those were good times."*

I've lost track of how many stories I've heard about my father since he passed in 2001. My brothers and I never knew about any of those random acts of kindness.

Not once did our dad sit down at the dinner table and tell us about his good deeds.

For 73 years, Dad had been sneaking around—being a nice guy behind our backs.

Clearly, he has passed the legacy test. My dad made people feel good about knowing him, about having him around. These people will never forget what he did for them and how he did it. These days, I get choked up every time I see a house with Christmas lights or a dusty chainsaw.

My mother had almost twenty more years to cement her legacy, yet, like Dad, she did it without forethought or intention.

Mom was beloved by everyone for her high energy and her easy laugh.

She was a careful listener who rarely offered advice. If she didn't know about something, she refused to pretend she did.

Her appetite for adventure was legendary. Mom's motto: "If someone asks to do something and you don't want to do it, do it anyway. It might be fun!"

And 'do it' she did.

She broke wild horses. She drove fast cars. She was a champion in her bowling league.

In her 40s she tried everything from barefoot water skiing to navigating long distance airplane trips to riding a motorcycle or jumping on a Segway mini. She was always excited to go hiking, fishing, camping, wear a funny costume or drive hundreds of miles to visit friends.

At 80, her face braved freezing water to bob for apples at my daughter Lauren's Halloween party.

By 89, she was still golfing with her girlfriends, organizing her Meals-For-One club, and meeting pals for exercise classes at the YWCA.

When she finally needed to move from her home to a memory care facility, she didn't complain. Instead, she coordinated an octogenarian breakfast club as a way to pull widows out of their shells. She was also the president of the Garden Club ("There are only two of us in the club, but I think I got voted in as President!")

If we reference Don Johnson's legacy test, Mom was a valedictorian. She never spoke about money or "things." She was unforgettable because she was generous with her time; doling out as much of it as possible to make anyone in her orbit feel important, loved, and happy.

I started this by saying there is still time to rewrite your tombstone. I asked Mom, "What do you want on your grave marker?" She was incredulous, "Nothing! I don't want to burden you boys with having to visit a monument. I won't be there anyway."

She wanted her ashes spread over Lake Shasta, California. She said, "We always had so much fun there." (We did the same for our father.)

When Mom was nearing the end of her life at 92, her spirit and sense of humor were fully intact. She had multiple visitors every day. Friends, children, grandchildren, and great grandchildren. She laughed long and loud at every joke. Hugs fell upon her as if she had her own inimitable gravitational pull.

Looking back, I never saw my mother in a bad mood.

I never heard her gossip or utter an unkind word about anyone.

I once asked her if she had any enemies. She thought for a

moment, "Do you know something…I don't. (big laugh) Besides, who has time for enemies?"

When my brothers and I asked her if she needed anything, her consistent response was, "I just wish I could see your dad again."

I have no doubt her wish was granted.

## What's In This For You?

*By all measures, your legacy is not improved by the amount of money you made or the monuments you carved. You will be remembered by how you made people feel. Will people say you were kind? Will they say you were generous with your time, your help, your love? Did you celebrate the achievements of others? If you cannot answer YES to those questions, you still have time to rewrite your tombstone. Speaking of legacy, this next story might prepare you to give a eulogy to honor someone you knew better than anyone.*

# CHAPTER 20

# Silent Goodbyes

*By Allison Dalvit*

### Why Read This Story?

*Were you ever asked to say a few words at a memorial on behalf of the dearly departed? Were your emotions so jumbled you couldn't say what you wanted? Then, this story may inspire you to pre-think your eulogy to comfort the living—even though you may never need it.*

In 2019, I buried the love of my life when he was only 57.

Sudden heart failure in front of his TV.

Tony Cacciavillani was an iron man of fitness, ethics, and character. His sudden death was an unfathomable occurrence nobody saw coming.

And now, at his celebration of life, I was expected to stand in front of the whole family, our loved ones, and our coworkers to deliver the perfect send off. I knew Tony better than anyone and yet…

I couldn't do it.

I was so unprepared for Tony's shocking death, so overwhelmed with pain, loss, sickness, and confusion that I couldn't put my thoughts and feelings into intelligible words. A proper eulogy was beyond my comprehension, on every possible level.

I've emceed hundreds of events and had spoken publicly to thousands of people. Why was this so impossible?

Maybe if I tell you more about this man, you'll "get it."

I fell in love with Tony when we both worked on a television set for the Food Network.

He was a cameraman. I was a producer. The days were long yet, as a young hot-shot team, we were totally in sync. Work was always fun together. He was single. I was newly divorced, but he never crossed the line with me; always treating me with a paragon of respect.

Over time, I started seeing Tony in a brighter light. I respected his reputation for extreme loyalty. I saw him as a charming hero who could save any day. To sweeten the deal, the physical attraction between us was undeniable.

A few months after we had fallen in love, Tony surprised me by setting up an elaborate beach vacation in Cancun, Mexico. The first night we arrived, he popped The Question.

I said YES! We were married later that year.

It was a thrilling start! The two of us were always rushing into things together. We couldn't slow down because we were too amped for the happily ever after.

My dad, a car guy, used to say that engines that run too hot, burn up quickly.

I guess that was what happened to us.

Our blended worlds came together like the Santa Ana winds hitting a forest fire. There were so many factors that torched our marriage that Tony and I divorced after just one year together. We loved each other very much but we just couldn't make the marriage function without flames. What surprised everyone was that we had the kindest divorce and remained best friends.

Even though we went our separate ways, we couldn't resist one another. The attraction was still palpable—but we were both stubborn. We fought a lot about big stuff and small stuff. We argued over stupid, tiny things. We would get together and have fun—and predictably piss each other off and walk away.

The confounding part was that it didn't matter if we were married, broken up, together as boyfriend and girlfriend, or we went through a period of being mortal enemies…in the end, we truly loved one another.

I've thought a lot about why we kept coming back to each other. It's incredibly simple.

There was never a betrayal. Regardless of our disagreements, we had nothing but mutual respect and honesty.

I also loved how Tony treated my daughters. He taught my girls how to drive. He made them waffles for breakfast. He showed up at all of their school events. After dinner, he loved to do all the dishes. He never missed a birthday or Christmas gift. He confided in my mom like a bestie and he became a close buddy with my dad. He took me to the doctor when I had a breast cancer scare. He didn't leave my side when I lost my father.

And, while the list is long in Tony's favor, he was also possessive, jealous, demanding, and had a big, loud personality. He could be the most difficult person in any room. Still, I couldn't stay away.

Almost ten years to the day after our divorce, in the summer of 2019, we decided to finally give our relationship another shot. Our children were a decade older. We were looking forward to finally getting 'our thing' right.

I was flying home from a trip and we'd made plans to meet for dinner. When I called him from the airport, Tony said he was exhausted from rebuilding his backyard fence. We made a date to connect later in the week.

That next night, Tony fell asleep watching TV and never woke up.

We didn't even know his death could have been prevented.

Tony was so busy micro-managing his Type 1 Diabetes, exercising regularly and making frequent doctor visits, that nobody considered his heart might be compromised. Tony was so confident in his longevity that he didn't even draft a will.

That's our story and why it was so difficult to explain at his celebration of life.

Maybe you know what I'm talking about.

Relationships like ours were complex.

I cannot tell you how many hundreds of times people would goad us—tell us we were so good together that we should remarry.

Much of what I've told you wasn't known by family, friends, or coworkers.

You know how it is. We don't talk about the rough patches we endure. We don't complain about the tears, the misgivings, and the doubts. We put on a good face right after we've just had a fight in the car.

Now you know why I couldn't find the right words at the right time. I was in pain and I was conflicted. I was angry and I was profoundly sad that Tony and I didn't get another chance. I left that day thinking I had let people down; the people who had come to celebrate the life of this complicated man.

I collected myself enough to write on Facebook what I wish I could have said in person.

Hundreds of photos and loving posts hit social media. Support and love for Tony was overwhelming. Everybody in the television production community shared stories of the difference Tony Cacciavillani had made in their lives.

My daughters gushed about what an incredible surrogate father he was...and what an impact he'd made on their future decisions.

Clayton Sandell (from ABC *World News Tonight*/*Good Morning America*) wrote multiple stories about his fierce friendship with Tony.

Finally, although it's been over a year since we all lost Tony, I am closer to finding peace with these last words:

*"Rest in peace, Tony. You were an amazing man, father, friend, cameraman, and a true love in my life. Thank you for the laughs, the love, and our wild crazy ride. You will be sorely missed—and I will love you forever and honor our time together.*

*I will hold down the fort, protect your children, and take care of any unfinished business you left behind...I've got your back."*

It took me some time to realize that eulogies are for the living. And, you know what? The living are just fine without your last words. They have their own memories. I also believe the loved one you lost wouldn't want you to suffer undue pain. When you can't eat or sleep, your loved one wouldn't want you to be tormented by the pressure of creating the perfect Hallmark moment.

## What's In This For You?

*If you should find yourself in a similar situation where you are expected to deliver the perfect memorial send off, you don't have to do it. It is okay to express your feelings on memorial pages, social media posts, or just reminiscing privately with friends. There is no wrong answer.*

*Tony Cacciavillani, a brilliant cameraman, husband, father, and friend. So sadly, he left us too soon. Tony's big personality is impossible to forget.*

# CHAPTER 21

# Follow Blueprints

*By Ross Shafer*

## Why Read This Story?

*If you are trapped in a dead-end job that is keeping you from getting what you want, this story will knock some sense into you.*

I'm dreadfully impatient.

Whenever I thought I deserved a promotion, whether I was qualified or not, I would figure out a way to get it.

When I saw something I wanted to buy, I wouldn't wait. I'd make it happen somehow.

Am I impulsive? How would I know? I never sit still long enough to fear the impossible.

I go after what I want because I know how to get it, every time. And I want you to know the secret, too.

To get what you want at light speed, you only need one thing.

Not drive.

Not money.

Not connections.

You need a shortcut.

Slow-minded people will tell you there are no shortcuts. These dream killers are hamstrung by the conventional wisdom, "You have to pay your dues and wait."

They're wrong!

Every accomplishment in life has a blueprint.

Building a house.

Sustaining a relationship.

Accruing a big bank account.

Climbing to the top of a career.

Sometimes you have to design the blueprint yourself, but I'll get to that in a moment.

If you can follow a blueprint that has been proven to work, you can accelerate the process of getting anything you want in this life.

I learned this in high school.

I liked girls. Girls liked football players. If I could play football, that appeared to be a shortcut for impressing girls...or at least getting them to notice me.

As a sophomore, I was a lean 160 pounds but had pretty good balance from riding dirt bikes. I tried out for the football team and made junior varsity.

No girls noticed me. I hadn't thought it through.

We played our games in broad daylight, after school, which meant no fans except our moms.

The big varsity game was played under tall Friday night lights with the marching band and bleachers full of girls.

I asked my PE coach, Joe Anderson, "How can I make it to the varsity squad?"

Coach Joe told me he had a "blueprint."

1. Put on 30 pounds of muscle. Lift weights four days a week.

2. Get faster by running 50-yard wind sprints on the school track.

3. The only TV shows you should watch are college or professional football games so you can learn how the game works.

I followed his blueprint religiously. By my junior year I was much faster. I was 6 feet tall and tipped the scales at a muscular 190 pounds. Because I had also studied the mechanics of the game from TV, I could "read" offensive plays and became a nimble tackler.

A couple of players on our team were being scouted by colleges, which meant lucrative scholarships. I was good but I wasn't being scouted. What was missing?

During one game, I saw a play unfold and I stuffed a 230-pound fullback at the line of scrimmage. My spine burned and went numb.

I'd suffered a stinger. A "stinger" is when two helmets crack together like two bull elk in rutting season.

I was pretty shaken up as I hobbled to the sideline.

My dad came down from the grandstand, crossed over the running track, to harangue me, "What are you doing here? You're not going to get a scholarship standing on the sidelines. You just gonna quit?"

My coach looked at me, "He's right. You've got to show some heart."

I had no idea what "showing heart" meant.

"Play through the pain," he said.

I went back in and, despite the pain, I tallied fifteen tackles and an interception.

I had a new step to add to my blueprint.

4.   If you feel like quitting, play through the pain anyway.

At the end of the season, I made 1st team All-Conference and got college scholarship offers to play football.

After four years of playing college football, I graduated with a B.A. in business management, but my impatience didn't fit in with most company cultures. I kept overachieving and asking for raises. But they couldn't pay me enough to buy the car I wanted.

I was complaining about this to my best friend and his dad overheard us. "You want money? You can buy all kinds of small businesses from the bankruptcy courts. You can get them for a song."

Really? Why?

"Because they're already broke."

I read up on the bankruptcy laws and he was right. I just needed to get around the one question the government clerks kept asking me, "Do you have any experience in running a business?"

I lied, "I'm hiring consultants to help me." From my football days, I concluded that all I needed was a successful blueprint.

I wound up buying a bankrupt mid-quality stereo store for $250. I say mid-quality because the previous owner didn't sell high-end McIntosh receivers or ear-splitting Klipschorn speakers. We sold Sanyo and Toshiba products. So, I renamed the store, *"Sounds O.K.,"* so customer's would manage their own expectations. *"Sounds O.K."* was a decent hit but the problem was this: Stereo gear only sold well at graduation and Christmas. We struggled the rest of the year. I needed to sell products that generated customers every day, like a gas station or a grocery store. I settled on the pet category. Dog and cat food. Pet toys. Fish and reptile accessories.

I was shocked to find out I could actually create a pet shop with zero money down. I bought a skeletal inventory on my credit card and built a second story over the Stereo department. *"Sounds O.K."* became *American's only Stereo and Pet Shop!* We painted a Parrot on the side of our delivery van and we got a little famous. My assistant manager, Gary, nicknamed us, *"Woofers and Tweeters."*

Unfortunately, I didn't know a cockatiel from a Cocker Spaniel, so I advertised in a free local paper (*Thrifty Nickel*) looking for a retired pet store manager to help me get it started. I found him! He was a funny older man (Tony Aprea) who worked in a music store during the day. At night he was happy to help a young guy like me. Tony told me what to buy and launched our store with credibility.

I bought a failing soup and sandwich shop for $100/week. I learned about portion control and thin-walled paper cups. But the rest seemed tricky, so I went to a sandwich convention and copied what worked in similar suburbs.

Can you see the pattern?

I repeated this system with a photography studio, an ice cream store, a T-shirt imprint company, flipping homes, and even as a big screen TV manufacturer.

If I didn't know how to run a certain business, I'd just exploit proven blueprints.

Ok, what do you do when you don't have a blueprint?

You create one.

When I was 27 years old, I went to a comedy club and loved it so much I wanted to switch careers. I'd written one joke that always got a laugh from my friends, *"I went to Los Angeles and saw the movie* Texas Chainsaw Massacre. *These Californians were terrified. I grew up in a logging town so when I saw the movie I thought, 'I can't believe they're using a McCulloch 210.'"*

I signed up for an open mic night to try out other jokes I'd written. The chain saw joke killed but everything else totally bombed. If I was going to get on a fast track as a paid comedian, I needed a blueprint.

Johnny Carson's *Tonight Show* was the gateway to a career in stand-up comedy. But how the hell was I going to make that happen?

Maybe there was a "science" to who got booked on that show?

I hired a stand-up comedy coach in Sebastopol, California named, Jim Richardson. Jim had videotaped every comedian who ever performed a solid 6-minute comedy spot on Johnny's show. I watched the tapes and used graph paper to tabulate how many laughs-per-minute they got during their "spot."

Johnny Carson liked comics who got six laughs per minute— with each laugh sustaining three seconds or more. Richardson helped me edit my jokes using the following blueprint. From hanging out at the clubs, I found that most new comedians only write a couple of new jokes a month, often keeping a lot of their bad jokes hoping the next audience will like them.

By contrast, I wrote hundreds of jokes a week and only kept the ones that followed "Johnny's formula." I threw out the duds.

Soon, my entire 40-minute club act had nothing but strong material. Within a year, I won an international comedy competition and was elevated to "headliner" status at comedy clubs. That led to touring with big name singing acts like Dionne Warwick, Dianna Ross, and Neil Sedaka.

With the support of established headliners and major nightclubs, the word got around that I was funny—and I was invited to do TV guest appearances. My comedy career allowed me to sell my other businesses.

What about making it to the coveted Johnny Carson show?

The week that Jim McCawley (Johnny's producer) thought I was finally ready for *The Tonight Show*, I got a big money offer to take over the Fox *Late Show* (after FOX let Joan Rivers go). My show directly competed with *The Tonight Show* so I never got to be on that show (although I got a couple of flattering handwritten notes from Johnny Carson).

I have been able to fast track every other business, career, and endeavor since then. I don't care if you are a plumber, a real estate agent, a schoolteacher, or a fish scaler…I promise you there is a blueprint waiting for you to shortcut whatever you want to achieve.

## What's In This For You?

*Proven blueprints are a shortcut to whatever you want to accomplish. Follow the path of someone successful and you don't have to reinvent the wheel.*

*A pet store consultant helped me create Sounds O.K. "America's Only Stereo and Pet Shop." His blueprint allowed me to understand how to make money in any business.*

*Following the blueprint of my high school coach Joe Anderson, I transformed from a 160 pound sophomore to a 190 pound senior who made 1st team all league. That status set me up for numerous college scholarship offers.*

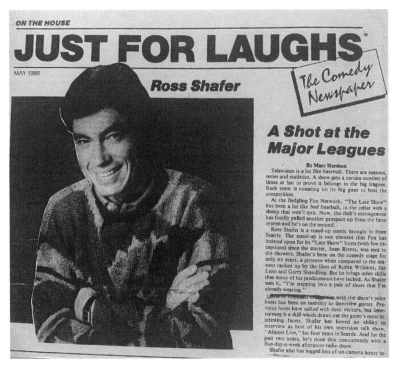

ON THE HOUSE

# JUST FOR LAUGHS®

MAY 1988

**Ross Shafer**

*The Comedy Newspaper*

## A Shot at the Major Leagues

**By Marc Hershon**

Television is a lot like baseball. There are seasons, series and statistics. A show gets a certain number of times at bat to prove it belongs in the big leagues. Each team is counting on its big guns to beat the competition.

At the fledgling Fox Network, "The Late Show" has been a lot like *bad* baseball, in the cellar with a slump that won't quit. Now, the club's management has finally pulled another prospect up from the farm system and he's on the mound.

Ross Shafer is a stand-up comic brought in from Seattle. The stand-up is one element that Fox has insisted upon for its "Late Show" hosts (with few exceptions) since the starter, Joan Rivers, was sent to the showers. Shafer's been on the comedy stage for only six years, a pittance when compared to the seasons racked up by the likes of Robin Williams, Jay Leno and Garry Shandling. But he brings other skills that many of his predecessors have lacked. As Shafer sees it, "I'm stepping into a pair of shoes that I'm already wearing."

One of the main difficulties with the show's prior hosts has been an inability to interview guests. Previous hosts have *talked* with their visitors, but *interviewing* is a skill which draws out the guest's most interesting facets. Shafer has honed an ability to interview as host of his own television talk show, "Almost Live," for four years in Seattle. And for the past two years, he's done that concurrently with a five-day-a-week afternoon radio show.

Shafer also has logged lots of on-camera hours be-

*With Jim Richardson's joke editing "blueprint," I was able to accelerate my stand-up comedy career from open-mic comic to Headline Act at the nation's top comedy venues. Before long, I was hosting network television shows.*

# CHAPTER 22

# Catch Dreams

*By Allison Dalvit*

## Why Read This Story?

*Are you going through a divorce? A serious break up?
Did your children witness a toxic relationship? Do you
wish you could make the pain go away by performing
a little distracting sleight of hand? Then, you will want
to read this story.*

My daughter Cass was an innocent six-year-old when her father
and I threw in the nuptial towel.

When I tried to explain to her why her dad and I couldn't live
together anymore she seemed totally disinterested. At six, maybe
mourning wasn't an emotion she gave much weight.

So, I dropped the subject and carried on.

Like most parents, I loved to settle in with my kids and read
bedtime stories. Some divorced parents think you should read
divorce-oriented books like, *Two Homes* or *Dinosaurs Divorce*.
I felt that would only shine a spotlight on the divorce instead of
minimizing it.

Besides, I didn't want to force books on her. I let Cass bring me stories that caught her fancy.

Cass's favorite book was *Arthur Goes to Camp.* She wanted me to read it to her every night. In her six-year-old mind, she would fantasize about putting on her own backpack, turning on her flashlight, and exploring a kid's camp just like Arthur. It was so cute.

Then, she wanted to turn up the heat on the fantasy.

She was convinced she should join Arthur at camp. I laughed and reminded her she was still my baby—way too young to go to a sleep-away camp. But Cass was a stubborn little person. She wasn't taking NO for an answer.

I thought I could dissuade Cass with a challenge. "If you want something really badly you need to pitch your ideas in a rational way." She nodded like she knew what the word 'rational' meant. Cass was an incredibly intelligent little girl who took her assignment seriously.

On "pitch day," Cassidy dressed up like a professional camper (little backpack, flashlight, baseball cap). In a cleverly organized sequence, she told me what she would do at camp (swim, ride horses, hike). She explained how her experience would benefit her life (make friends, learn new skills). Then, she wrapped it all up with her form of rationale, "Mom, it's so I can be a kid."

She knew exactly the right words to crack me. With all of the adult divorce nonsense happening, more than anything, I wanted what Cassidy wanted—we both just wanted her to be a kid.

Unbeknownst to her, I had been secretly researching kids' camps. To give myself one more escape route, I told her, "Before

I make a decision, we should visit an actual kids' camp."

She asked, "When, mommy?"

I said, "Today!"

She squealed! My only concern now was Cass might cry if Arthur wasn't in the driveway to welcome her.

(Sing with me parents) "Over the river and through the woods...off to camp we go!"

Camp Geneva Glen was the closest camp to our home (a mere 20 minutes away). It was a small camp that offered two-week sessions. I couldn't imagine being away from my tiny daughter for that long, so I kept telling myself the tour was just a self-contained adventure in itself. If the camp was too over-whelming, I'd be there to talk her off the ledge.

We arrived at the camp and started our tour. It was a rainy day but that didn't stop Cass from clomping through the mud to see the crafts, the horses, and the archery range.

For me, Camp GG was clean and kid friendly. Cozy little cabins spread out over the mountainside. The aroma of southern fried chicken salted the air.

For Cassidy, Camp GG was a wonderland of fairy dust, friendships, and magic wands. Without saying a word to each other, we synced on one thought, "This is the perfect place for a kid to be a kid."

I was softening.

However, a meeting with the camp director, Nancy, didn't sound hopeful. "We have generations of campers—alumni—legacy—and to be honest it's extremely difficult to get in." Hard to say who looked saddest, Cass or me.

Then, Nancy revealed there was one child who didn't show up and Cass could jump into that spot, today! I freaked out! Could I really leave my baby girl at a sleep-away camp for the next two weeks? What kind of mom would that make me?

With her full pack still on her back, Cass looked up at me with her beautiful big hazel eyes, and smiled so wide I could see the sunshine, "Mommy, I'm staying."

Nancy piped in, "Don't worry. You have time to get what she needs while I take her to her chicken dinner."

This idea was taking on a life of its own. I felt pulled into Nancy's vortex as I took her giant list of camping paraphernalia and raced to a sporting goods store to get Cass's first sleeping bag, a pair of tiny hiking books, rain gear, and whatever else filled the list.

After tonight, Cass would officially become a happy camper, just like Arthur.

By contrast, I would be a wreck.

For my own sanity, I became a de facto double agent, 'casing the camp' from afar.

Each day, I found a good spot on the hill across from camp, my car facing the compound. I would only leave if I caught a glimpse of my little girl having fun.

Daily, I would invent any excuse to hand-deliver goodie bags. Eventually, the camp asked me to stop. From then on, I was told I needed to use the post office to mail my "care packages."

So, of course, I did.

I also included addressed envelopes and stationery so Cass could write to her mommy. Over the two weeks I got a total of two letters. THE BEST!

When the two weeks were finally over, I was the first parent in the lot for pick up.

I was over an hour early. (The camp didn't quite know what to do with me.)

When Cass finally jumped in the car, she acted like I'd dropped her off yesterday. She couldn't wait to show me the wands she'd made (twigs with glitter glued on the ends). She told me stories about her hilarious cabinmates. She recited the lessons she learned from her camp counselors. And, she couldn't stop swelling with pride over the adventures she conquered.

From that summer on, Cass attended Camp Geneva Glen every year until she was old enough to become a camp counselor herself.

She wanted to be "a part of making the magic that lets kids be kids."

To this day, campers still reach out to Cass to thank her for sitting next to them through homesickness and archery awards. She is still best friends with the counselors she befriended at Camp Geneva Glen.

Her life was so full of joy from Arthur's original inspiration that she never once asked about the details of our divorce.

## What's In This For You?

*As adults who split from our mates, we assume our children will suffer the loss with the same depth of pain that we do. We forget that they are, first and foremost, children who just want the space and freedom to play, to laugh and to make friends. Don't bog them down with your "ex drama." Instead, let them roll in the mud. Let them live out fantasies. Let them climb things. Dress them up in costumes. Remind them how smart they are when they crush a challenge. These are the magic tricks that bring joy to a childhood.*

*6-year-old Cass "pitched her case" to me about attending Camp Geneva Glen.*

*The camp lessons and adventures inspired Cass to become a camp counselor during High School and College.*

*Here, my mom and I got to set up her cabin and sleeping quarters.*

# CHAPTER 23

# Start Over

*By Ross Shafer*

## Why Read This Story?

*If you are "of a certain age" (35, 40, 45, 50+) and worried about the end game, this story is for you.*

Did you wake up today trapped by what your friends and family define as having "a pretty good career"?

On the outside, you appear to live well—you have a cool home, two cars, your children are well-dressed and in a good school. You haven't quite pulled the trigger on a vacation property but at least you've got an upscale latte machine and an eco-friendly electric lawn mower.

But damn, you thought you'd be saving more money by now.

You thought you would ascend to a destination of rank and power. Inside, you question if you made a bad choice five years ago. You might even be angry with yourself for turning down a job that would have made you rich.

You still think the grass is greener elsewhere, but the thought of changing companies—or worse, careers—is scary as hell.

Do you find yourself asking your friends to scope out work for you? "Hey, if you hear of a job I might like, drop my name. But keep it on the down low."

How will you break the news of you changing jobs…to… everyone you know?

I can hear your stomach roiling from here; because all of that has happened to me.

At 40, I had an escalating network TV career, hosting talk and game shows on NBC, ABC, FOX, CBS, and USA.

I was "connected" and had a very bright future…right up until I didn't. After five cancellations and suspicious changes in management, I was summarily dismissed; younger faces got the work as I bounced to the street to start over from scratch.

Like you, I had the house, the pool, the kids, the cars, the wine club membership, and the terrifying prospect of not being able to pay for what seemed like panoramic bills.

At first, I tried to retain my lifestyle for posturing purposes— also to keep my high maintenance wife from freaking the hell out. A peer of mine whispered, "Success is perception, brother. Success begets success." I didn't know what "beget" meant but I put my back into that facade hard, until I realized perception wouldn't keep my pool heated.

After I lost my house and my impatient wife, I was forced to cede to reality. I defaulted to a studio apartment and a 14-year-old Mazda 626 wagon.

Embarrassed, I hid from people.

I didn't return phone calls.

Still relatively young, I was faced with the distinct probability of outliving myself.

My ego had to die so I could plot out my remaining fifty-year future.

If this sounds like you, I urge you to confront reality sooner than I did.

Assume you are forced to reinvent your life. Where do you start?

Sit alone and take an inventory of your marketable skills. List your experience, your accomplishments, your hobbies, your friends, your nascent avocations, even your long-lost interests that have lain dormant since you took the job that now betrays your future.

People have asked me, "With your pedigree, couldn't you just wait for another TV show?"

Wait? How long? Six months? A year? Two years?

Every day, that Mazda reminded me I didn't have the financial froth to wait, even a month.

My list: I had been a successful touring stand-up comedian making five grand a week. No good. The comedy club boom died with the advent of TV shows like *Evening at the Improv*, *The A-List*, and *The Laugh Factory*. Watching comedians on TV, for free, killed the live club business. The big name acts I'd toured with were retiring. After five TV show cancellations, my TV agent wouldn't return my calls. Show business forgot to inform me I was no longer a member.

Go back farther, Ross.

When I was in my 20s, I was young and fearless. I bought and sold small businesses out of bankruptcy. Two dozen of them.

What if I turned those adventures into lessons? Make them funny? Could I actually sell stories like that to anybody?

I contacted Kiwanis clubs, Elks Lodges, Chambers of Commerce, and I reached out to corporate leaders I had come to know. I asked if I could entertain the members at their meetings for free. After about a year, I discovered some meetings would pay me to tell stories and jokes.

A rocky start, but eventually, I morphed my "talents" into a profitable new career as a professional keynote speaker.

It's been 21 years. Ten books. Almost 3,000 corporate engagements. Sixteen human resource training films. I took responsibility for my next unforeseen career, and I never had to be dependent on anyone again.

Don't let your age or circumstances deceive you into thinking a career change is suicide. The fear you feel is temporary.

When I sat in the dark, alone, dreading my empty future, a friend of mine, Jay Leno, swathed me in stories about older people who had changed careers past 50.

Frank McCourt was a retired schoolteacher. At 65, he tried to write a novel. His book *Angela's Ashes* sold over eight million copies and won the Pulitzer Prize.

Mother Teresa of Calcutta won the Nobel Peace Prize at 69 and because she had so much energy, she worked full time until she was 87.

Frenchman Peter Roget suffered from obsessive compulsive disorder. His doctor found that the only thing that calmed Peter down was making random lists of things. One of his lists involved thinking of different words that meant the same thing. At 73,

Roget published a product we've all used—*Roget's Thesaurus*.

I am sympathetic that you don't know what you will do…or how you will pull it off. But that's ok. Make that list of your skills, talents, and experience. Research how to sell those talents and experience.

If you are frustrated or your job prospects have fallen away (like mine did), dedicate yourself to learning how to speak and present yourself well to others through a tiny computer camera. If you can do that, you will be able to sell your valuable knowledge and services online.

In fact, today might be the best time in your history to think about changing careers. Communicating during the Covid-19 pandemic proved to all of us that we can accomplish miracles via Zoom, Skype, Microsoft Teams, Google Hangouts, and other video conferencing services.

Teleconferencing is a boon for gig workers and independent consultants. Learn how to use your computer to open up your new life.

## What's In This For You?

*I've been exactly where you are. After speaking to several million people in 35 years, I know your best life lies ahead. You just have to believe there is no age limit on enthusiasm. Wisdom does not "age-out." Don't psyche yourself out over your next chapter, even if you don't know what that is. Plenty of people have done their best work after 50. I know I sound like a motivational speaker, but I don't care. I've lived it and I'm right.*

*From Comedy Clubs and Casinos to Corporate Stages all over the world taught me how to reinvent on demand.*

# CHAPTER 24

# Protect Yourself

*By Allison Dalvit*

## Why Read This Story?

*Even if you think you have a good job, I don't want you to be blindsided when you are told your company is going under. I don't want you to lose your home because you found out a gig worker was hired to take over your responsibilities. Are you freaking out because you don't have a backup plan? Read on.*

*Only the Paranoid Survive* is the title of former Intel CEO Andy Grove's book. Andy was making the point that, if we get too comfortable, none of our jobs are safe.

I never read Andy Grove's book, but I agree with the premise.

Not having enough money scared me into insomnia; especially since I had chosen a high-risk, low-security career.

After getting my degree in journalism, I had been blinded by the glamour of working in television news. I took almost every dangerous, low-paying gig I could find in my quest to build a credible resume. I scratched my way to the top of my profession, which was still no guarantee of financial comfort. Every highly experienced cohort of mine sat by the phone every day waiting for a new assignment.

I loved the work, but I knew I was walking a tightrope.

I also knew I wanted to have babies.

It dawned on me that I had better create a PLAN B financial safety net.

Where should I start? What could I do?

I watched (and later worked on) HGTV "fix and flip" shows and saw other people make money by improving real estate. Maybe I could do that? My only roadblock to riches was I didn't have enough money for a down payment on a house.

I was also in the middle of a high-risk pregnancy with my second child Mikaela.

Her little life was hanging by a thread, and I had to be put on bedrest for several months.

Lying in bed waiting for my daughter's arrival, I learned all about stock market day trading. It was a good fit. It was "working without moving."

I had a little money saved so I experimented.

Pretty soon, I figured out how to buy a stock low and sell it for a profit—all within a few minutes or hours. I rarely kept a stock longer than a day. Then, I'd take my profits off the table and put that money in a savings account.

Rinse and repeat.

This went on for four to five months.

The only time I had to cash in my chips was when I needed to be present for an emergency C-section with Mikaela!

I was not about to relax and let my money ride—without

paying attention.

As it turned out, my labor with Mikaela practically coincided with the implosion of the dot.com economy.

Was my "getting out" a matter of luck? I don't think so.

I had become so disciplined I knew it was foolish to simply trust the stock market's stability. That would be the equivalent of driving in an ice storm and taking your hands off the steering wheel.

I was so focused on saving the life of my preemie that I didn't even examine the details of my bank account until after she was safe and growing normally.

With Mikaela out of the woods, I was pleasantly surprised when I saw I had enough money to buy my first rental investment property.

Let's review.

I was in a shaky freelance career.

I didn't have a money coach.

I didn't have a trust fund.

I simply had the desire to protect my financial future, and the discipline to learn a new "trade" on the off chance my Plan A television career tanked.

You be me for a minute.

If you really want to create your own PLAN B source of income, don't use "I don't have the money" as an excuse. Start with whatever you have. I know people who make extra money selling items at garage sales, on Craigslist and eBay. Ross used to buy broken companies with zero money down, fix them up, and resell them.

Instead of being left with no money, I hope you are frightened enough to secure your own future. If you are determined to protect yourself with a PLAN B source of income, start small and make small moves until you reach the first tier of your goal. Then you'll feel what it's like to put your money to work for you.

Back to our story.

With the little extra dough I'd saved, I bought a studio condo in Breckenridge, Colorado. It was only 400 square feet and the bed came out of the wall. The location was at the bottom of a ski-lift. My plan was to rent the place to ski bums.

I couldn't afford to hire a handyman so I brought my young kids with me to rip off dated wallpaper, repaint the walls, and decorate it, to the point that a rental company would list my unit. It was a scary risk for me until I discovered this little property allowed me to make a steady rental income while it grew in value.

Then, when the timing was right, I sold the condo for a profit and rolled it into a bigger property in a better location.

I've done that over and over again…for twenty years.

My backup plan has made it possible for this single mom to put both of her daughters through college, without the pressure of relying on one volatile job to provide everything.

The funny irony of this "side hustle" was that my PLAN B more than replaced my PLAN A career. I no longer had to take the TV jobs that were located in swamps, shot in dangerous locations, or covering bizarre stories you'd never want to see on TV anyway.

I found security in something else. Something I wasn't even officially trained to do.

## What's In This For You?

*Do you wake up every day worried about losing your job? Do you think your newly diagnosed high blood pressure and bleeding ulcer are a result of that stress? Then, start thinking about mapping out your own backup plan. Ultimately, you are the only person responsible for staying employed. Explore all of your options…and don't let me catch you saying you don't have the money or the time to protect yourself.*

# CHAPTER 25

# Enter Contests

*By Ross Shafer*

## Why Read This Story?

*Did you receive your first certificate or trophy for learning to swim? Selling Girl Scout cookies? Winning the soccer championship? Did you enter a contest for the best Halloween costume? Would you like to return to those times when your friends and family gathered around you to validate your success? This story will teach you how to find that feeling whenever you want it.*

I always thought it was cool to enter contests. But it took me a while to understand the power of winning them.

I discovered winning any kind of award made me forget about the insecurities that paralyzed me as a child.

What insecurities?

I am pretty sure my lack of confidence started when the cutest girl in my third grade class, Jackie Harper, told me I had a big, square head.

In fourth grade, my mother told me I could only wear "husky

boy" jeans because, for a nine-year-old at 85 pounds, I was getting too fat.

The next year, my father stopped taking me fishing because he said my talking too much scared the fish away.

At 11, I loved playing catcher on the baseball team. That is, until a teammate's dad yelled at me from the bleachers, "Shafer has a weenie arm! He can't even throw to second base."

I quit fishing. I quit baseball. I quit eating. After all, I was a chubby, large-headed, talkative little boy.

My mother, seeing me mope at our annual family reunion in Salem, Oregon, urged me to enter a potato sack race against my nine older cousins. I was the tubby one—and the most mocked. My Uncle Fred yelled, "I don't think they make potato sacks in your size."

My face got so red from anger that I out-bounced everyone. I was swarmed with pats on my back. First prize was Aunt Ella's Boston cream pie. I ate more than half of it.

None of my clan had any clue how unworthy I felt inside, but the lesson was permanent.

I associated winning with earning respect.

From that day through adulthood, winning became my job. I would research the award I wanted, study the habits of previous award winners, and then out-work my competition to snatch the prize.

In fifth grade I won the $25 first prize for reading 201 books. I got a certificate and was asked to give an oral report at the Friday assembly. The prettiest girl in sixth grade told me I was the smartest boy at New Hayesville Elementary. Not once, did she mention my head size.

In high school, I was elected student body president.

As a senior, I made the 1st Team All-League football team and played in the Shriner's Bowl. Football scholarships followed.

My obsession with winning replaced my insecurities with something previously unfamiliar to me—confidence.

I used my meager savings to buy dilapidated homes and bankrupt businesses. Creating "America's Only Stereo & Pet Shop" led to a weird campaign that awarded me with ten-thousand dollars in free publicity.

In the wake of my greatest hits, my mother and father kept me humble. Dad said, "I love you son, but you're not that important. If I were you, I'd stop bragging about yourself all the time."

When I was 24, my dad told me, "You make every conversation all about you. That's what insecure people do." I was so impressed with myself, I didn't even realize I was doing it.

I was able to turn a profit from just about any business, but I was bored.

One night, I had an epiphany at a local comedy club.

I saw comedians getting laughs, which I interpreted as a large audience accepting them. And because I'm a moth drawn to that kind of flame I decided to try stand-up comedy myself.

(Heads up: I'm going to ignore my dad's humility reminder for just a moment to insert shameless braggadocio...but you'll get over it in a minute.)

Two years later, using my study and practice tactics, I ascended through the smokiest of nightclubs to win the $5,000 first prize in an international stand-up comedy competition.

Immediately, I started touring the country as a headliner.

The next logical step was to tell my jokes on TV—first as a comedy guest and then as the host of my own talk show. I got on all the top comedy shows of the day and won numerous Emmy awards.

Look out—the award-winning boasting continues…

I won the Iris Award for creating the best comedy television show in America.

I became the host of four network television talk and game shows.

When I was cancelled by all four network television shows, I switched careers and started writing business books (two bestsellers) and won the CPAE Hall of Fame award in the world of professional public speaking.

I jotted down that list because I want you to know that you don't have to wait around to win an award. Winning, the way I did it, was methodical and intentional. Whenever I shifted to a new career, I researched which awards garnered the most respect.

By studying award winners, it became obvious to me that recognition was good for dissolving deeply held insecurities like anxiety, fear, and sadness.

Recognition builds confidence.

Recognition changes the way the world sees you.

Award winners also earn more money, get more opportunities, and often enjoy the admiration of their peers, family, and employers.

That's why I believe you can restore that rewarding feeling of accomplishment you had as a kid.

Every industry rewards people who work hard (because awards inspire others to work harder, too).

Dedicate yourself to turning in better work than your coworkers and competitors. The awards will find you.

In sales, it's easy to see where you rank on the leader board. Study who's on top and replicate what they do. Sell more and you'll work your way up the board.

In engineering or architecture, which people and companies are winning the bids? Who is winning the design awards? Study their processes and originality. Imitate the process. Awards will follow.

In the entertainment business, who is winning a Grammy, a Tony, an Emmy, or an Oscar? I'll blow the lid off this for you. The winners are methodically choosing material they know will move people, emotionally. Then, if that person can be original in his/her interpretation of that material, a trophy will go to the person who drew the most tears.

Ok, if intentionally seeking awards does not make you feel comfortable, yet you see the career advantages for winning them, then you can take a passive approach and still win awards.

Awards are given for philanthropy (giving your money away).

Awards are given for volunteering your time to charity organizations.

Awards are given for longevity (as in, lifetime achievement awards).

Awards are given for good deeds. At least one television station in your town has an annual hero award for bravery and/or kindness.

Almost every local city magazine publishes profiles on people and companies who simply serve the best tasting product or provide the most reliable service.

Sometimes the magazine will hear about a candidate from fans. Other times, a new business may be required to pay a nomination fee. Look for these annual awards.

Which company makes the best cheeseburger?

Who makes the best cup of coffee?

Who is the best hair stylist?

Who is the best realtor?

Who is the best dentist?

Who provides the best customer service?

You get the idea. And, do you know what happens next?

The best are now distanced from the rest…from the ordinary.

Ratings and awards count in this reputation economy.

Awards change your life.

## What's In This For You?

*I don't care why you want to win awards. To boost your self-esteem? Show off your talents? Make more money? Enhance your sex appeal? Make your family proud? Create a kind of "insurance policy" to ensure a long career? Regardless of your reasons, I applaud your desire to be heralded. Besides, winning is much better than watching some sub-par person walk off with <u>your</u> award.*

# CHAPTER 26

# Confront Conflicts

*By Allison Dalvit*

## Why Read This Story?

*By now you have all heard about the #MeToo movement. It is a rallying cry to restore power to innocent women who have been exposed to sexual harassment and sexual abuse by powerful and/or prominent men. Even we women are often surprised by how many of our friends have been victimized. Read this and realize that <u>you</u> can change this.*

I've been chased around more desks than you can buy at an Office Depot.

See, just then, I defaulted to making a joke about it.

When I think about how we women dealt with inappropriate sexual advances in the 90s, I'm saddened. The majority of us didn't complain. We didn't speak up. We didn't rock the boat. We tried to play it down, laugh it off, make excuses, or quit the best job of our lives and stay quiet.

When did sexual harassment start for me?

At 16 years old, my retail store manager called me into the back office to show me that he liked wearing women's underwear. He pulled his pants down so I could see. I was frozen with fear. When I mentioned it to the store's owner, the job got weird. Did they fire the cross-dressing manager? No. The only adjustment the owner made was to not let us work the same shifts anymore. Thankfully, a few months later, I was off to college and left that job anyway.

At 17, I was a server at a well-known restaurant chain when a customer asked if I was on the menu. I told my boss. His remedy was to tell me, "Get used to it!"

So I quit.

I was pretty bummed out because it was a popular restaurant and everybody in my high school wanted to work there.

Before I go on, I want to stop you in your tracks if you think any of this was my fault. I never wore seductive clothing, too much makeup, quietly flirted, or flat out "asked for it."

That assumption is categorically NOT TRUE.

I was never "sexy" at work and I never relied upon "being female" to advance in any career. If you read any of the other stories in this book you will know that I worked my ass off to be competent and worthy of my job(s). Not once did I use my sexuality as a shortcut or advantage. If I did, I would probably still be working there. Instead, I quit every job where I felt harassed. Furthermore, I never blew the whistle.

No woman I know would ever make up these kinds of stories.

If we drew attention to any form of sexual impropriety, we women would be castigated as victims and troublemakers. We would be punished for calling out behaviors that were tanta-mount to blackmail. Our true motives were to earn money, buy food, shelter, and raise our families.

Let me ask you, would you continue to work for the follow-ing men?

I was told by a married boss that he had fallen in love with me. To deflect his advances, I made up a story—telling him it took one full year/365 days to fall in love.

His response was to write the number 365 on his office whiteboard. We had our daily meetings in there. He used the number as a countdown clock and referenced it in our morning meetings. He changed the numbers daily...364, 363, 362 and so on. I cringed, hoping the rest of my team didn't catch on. At one point, he pulled me away from work to "shop" for a second home in the city for him...and me. I wanted to die! When the count-down clock got closer to the one-year mark, I had no choice but to start a new job hunt.

A major government official asked me to sit on his lap if I wanted to get a "good interview."

I was invited to participate in my supervisor's swingers club. He described how the men in his group would throw their car keys in a bucket and the women would grab a random key. That is who they would sleep with that night. My eyes bugged out of my head with shock. When I told him swinging wasn't my thing, he felt judged and made my job hell. I had to quit.

I've often thought about where I would rank on the company ladder if I'd had the luxury of building my career with just one company, and no threat of sexual harassment.

The sad truth of #MeToo statistics is that one-third of women worldwide (according to #MeToo founder, Tarana Burke) have faced some level of sexual harassment from someone in a position of power. As a single mom raising two daughters, I didn't have the resources or the career options to fight it. I did know that if I "narced" on a boss, that would be the end of my job. I would be blacklisted and unable to work in that industry. For sure, I would get labeled a "problem."

This behavior was kept under wraps for so long because we women didn't talk about it amongst ourselves.

In 2017, sick feelings in my stomach came flooding back when I was asked to field produce the Taylor Swift sexual harassment trial for E! Entertainment News. The trial stemmed from a sexual assault incident in 2013.

This was a huge moment in the #MeToo movement.

A local Denver country radio station DJ, David Mueller, was accused of reaching his hand up Swift's skirt and groping her butt at a pre-concert meet and greet. Mueller was fired and now asking for $3 million in damages.

Swift countersued for $1. She didn't want money or publicity; she wanted justice and awareness for sexual assault and the #MeToo movement.

Taylor Swift had an advantage. She was young, talented, and famous. Fans snap countless pictures of "Tay Tay."

In court, Swift submitted a high-resolution photograph showing Mueller's hand exactly where she said it was. Swift won!

Taylor Swift speaking up attracted a cascade of attention to the #MeToo movement, and many of us are eternally grateful.

But I don't want to dismiss or minimize the millions of women who didn't get their day in court...who weren't rich...who weren't famous...yet were traumatized for life because they were violated and had to quietly bury their pain.

It is too late for me to name the names of creeps who made my working years uncomfortable. I don't have to. You know who you are. I guarantee if something like this ever happens to me again, you better believe I will go public.

I want to live in a world where my daughters don't have to deal with sexual harassment, assault, or unwelcome advances.

## What's In This For You?

*#MeToo still has a long way to go. But the impact of this movement is undeniable. The world has opened its eyes to how widespread this issue has become—across every business industry, countless public and government service organizations, seemingly innocent non-profit entities, and even the churches and synagogues we are expected to trust. You can be cautious. But you don't have to stay silent. You don't have to be a victim.*

*It was exciting yet emotional to cover the Taylor Swift sexual harass-
ment trial for E! Entertainment television. The office building across
the street from the Denver courthouse put up daily post-it note messages of encouragement that echoed Taylor's song lyrics.*

# CHAPTER 27

# Bury Cliches

*By Ross Shafer*

## Why Read This Story?
*This story is about rethinking what you have been taught. You don't need to live by the motivational quotes you've posted on your office wall or read on social media.*

There is an entire industry built on false promises.

That industry sells landscape-enhanced pithy motivational posters. Now, we see them reposted and retweeted on social media platforms.

As a former football player, my coach posted these laconic mind twisters in our locker room. I'd bet your boss has probably mounted several of them in your break room.

I admit, I have always had a relentless thirst for inspirational messages. But when I started to use these pearls myself, it was devastating to learn that my favorite quotes were empty and naïve.

## Success Is About Who You Know
This message is about the power of "connection." Allegedly telling you that your success is tied to making friends with people

who can give you a leg-up in your personal and professional life.

Don't buy it. Making connections with people who are eager to help you is a fantasy. The people you want to connect with are busy. Besides, what do you have to offer them? Nothing yet? Then why would they spend their valuable time curating your career? The superstars you think will change your life don't have time to mentor you.

More importantly you don't have to wait to make friends with powerful people.

The more realistic quote is one I coined, "SUCCESS IS ABOUT WHO KNOWS YOU."

Instead of waiting for the perfect mentor to open doors for you, dedicate your energy to becoming exceptional at something.

People who are exceptional at something don't need other people to make connections for them. Exceptional people get noticed by their own efforts—and are able to accelerate their own paths in life. Sorry, nobody else can build a life for you…except you.

You need to be the person others want to connect with.

You need to know your profession well enough to unearth original insights.

You need to be consistent—so you earn the title of the go-to source in your field.

Now go take down that poster.

## Fake It Until You Make It

This is complete nonsense.

I first heard this quote from a well-known marriage counselor who was encouraging my wife and I to pretend to like each other.

The "expert" was actually promoting fraudulent, inauthentic actions in order to restore emotions as complex as love and respect.

Faking behavior is never a solid plan. You'll be a fraud because you won't feel it, which means others will see through you as the phony you are.

By the way, faking it didn't save my rocky marriage. Faking expertise in your career might be worse. Eventually, counterfeit anything will only lead to discrediting the sliver of truth you have left.

## Don't Take No For An Answer

That slogan is supposed to inspire you to "never give up."

Nope. I think this phrase is trying to convince you that "achievement happens when you are annoying."

I love to buy stuff—but I hate being "sold."

Most people know what they want and what they don't want. If you don't take NO for an answer and you badger them, they will push back. No amount of persistence or pressure will change a smart person's mind.

Don't get me wrong, NO is a hard concept to accept.

Sadly, we can't get everything we want, whenever we want it. Success in this life has more to do with how you handle rejection than how you celebrate a sale. Rejection is good. Feeling unsuccessful teaches you how to bounce back from defeat.

If you are one of those people who crumbles easily over rejection, you will end up in a shrink's office getting advice from the "fake it 'til you make it" crowd.

Instead, look at that quote upside down:

## "Don't Take Yes For An Answer!"

If you can get past the NO's you will enjoy nurturing the YES's.

You might hear a "Yes" from a client, a customer, or your significant other. But wise people know that circumstances can change. YES can evolve into NO in an instant.

"My old boyfriend apologized for being a jerk and I want to give him another chance."

"My budget was just cut and I can't buy from you now. "

"We have decided to go in another direction, but I'll keep your number."

YES just means, for right now, the game is on.

Imagine you finally ask your girlfriend or boyfriend to marry you. He/She says "YES!" and you are elated by the victory. You have worked hard to be the perfect partner and now you think a license and ceremony will lock in the deal. The sale was made. No other effort required.

My friend, you are an idiot. How long do you think a neglected marriage will last?

To create a long-lasting relationship, personally or professionally, you'll need to curate the process. YES means you need to pay extra attention to the other party. YES means you will need to go above and beyond your competitors (or other suitors) to earn your intended's trust for a long-term relationship.

## What Doesn't Kill Us Makes Us Stronger

Are you kidding me?

I'd say something that almost kills you will at least scar you for life, if not leave you with a twitching case of PTSD.

How about using better judgment and NOT putting yourself in positions where you might endure extreme pain and anguish or potential death? I get that we all can be blindsided by death, loss, and boneheaded blunders by others—but I've learned to pre-assess my pain risks before I allow myself to be incapacitated by life.

The most important woman in my life was my hilarious and kind mother who passed away at 92. I knew losing her was going to be impossible to imagine. So, I pre-assessed the eventual pain, 25 years in advance. When she was 67 (after her triple bypass surgery), I made sure there was perfect clarity about how grateful I was to have her as my mom. When the day finally came that she booked a first-class seat to heaven, she and I only had joy. No regrets. It was knowing her that made me stronger—not recovering from the painful loss of her passing.

## What's In This For You?

*Don't be seduced by beautiful posters with cursive words that appear to unlock the keys to life. Don't assume these words are useful until you take them for a test drive in your own life. For 20 years, I've been hired as a personal growth speaker, consultant, and author. I've found that many of these citations aren't worth the 40# poster paper they were printed on. You can do better on your own.*

# CHAPTER 28

# Deny Arrogance

*By Allison Dalvit*

## Why Read This Story?

*Have you ever wondered why some of the people you admire still fail? Once you know why, you'll know how to sidestep the common trap that takes them down.*

Many of you buy a book like this to learn how to achieve "Best in Class" status. You hope being the best will attract money, fame, and opportunity.

WARNING: If you become the best—and get sloppy—hungry underdogs might use that moment to topple you.

I saw it when I worked on the set of the Food Network's show called *Challenge*. The episode theme: "Donut Champions."

Four donut bakers were challenged to fry up their original donut recipes in a do-or-die competition. The winner would walk away with donut glory and a big fat check for $10,000.

I was working as the field producer for one of four kitchens.

One of my bakers was the bona-fide donut superstar Mark Klebeck. He became famous when he struck a deal for his donuts to be sold in 15,000 Starbucks coffee stores.

By the time Mark glided into our soundstage, he was so rich and famous that he was no longer mixing the donut dough himself. Lucky for us, he was eager to share his experience and his success story.

The other three donut bakers were awestruck knowing they were baking against "The King" as many liked to call him.

The non-famous contestants owned mom-n-pop shops and were hoping to get enough exposure to escape donut obscurity.

Camera #1 was isolated on our oversized studio clock as it ticked toward show time.

The amateurs triple-checked their formulas.

Mark set about mixing, beaming with self-confidence. He was even unafraid to reveal his winning strategy: 1. Perfectly measured ingredients. 2. Knead plenty of air into the dough. 3. Do not overcook. He was delighted to be my color commentator; after all, he was "The King."

But there was another calm soul in the room.

Sara Beth Russert was a trendy, young and exceedingly focused donut baker from Seattle. Her specialty was confined to creating tasty vegan donuts.

The drama of pitting "Vegan Sara" against "The King" was delicious. Viewers always love a David vs. Goliath story.

Time was running out on the mixing round. Mark was now ready to fry up his dough. Cocksure, he eased the donut shapes into the hot oil as if to say, "This is how it's done, sister."

Suddenly, Mark's eyes telegraphed something was wrong.

Then we all saw it.

He had forgotten to insert the fryer basket. How could he

neglect to use the tool that lifts the donuts from the boiling oil?!

Three cameras zoomed in. My producer yelled into my headset, "Get him to explain his mistake!"

Mark beat me to the blunder.

He told a nationwide audience, "I made a rookie mistake and forgot to insert the basket, but I've got this."

He began another batch from scratch. As the consummate pro, Mark could hustle. The cooking segment timed out.

With $10,000 and bragging rights at stake, the judges took their time considering taste and texture. I thought I saw one of them give "The King" a wink. An almost imperceptible smile crept from the corner of Mark's lips.

His smirk vanished when the judges announced Sara won.

All judges agreed her vegan donut was delicious!

She flashed a thumbs up toward Mark and she graciously accepted her prize money.

The story of her nationally recognized vegan donuts glowed across the pages of the Seattle newspapers and elevated Mighty-O Donuts to world-class status.

Mark later wrote the book, *Top Pot Hand-Forged Doughnuts*, in which he humbly shared his secret recipes. He thanked his peeps from CNBC, The Travel Channel, *Fortune* magazine, and even yours truly got a shout out in the thanks section: "Allison Dalvit at *Food Network Challenge* for pushing me to compete."

## What's In This For You?

*When you are highly skilled and make a "rookie mistake," how do you handle it? Do you demonstrate grace under fire like Mark? Or do you beat yourself up and take your anger out on those around you? Often what separates the best from the ordinary is simply an error-free outcome. Does that describe you...or someone you would like to be?*

# CHAPTER 29

# Choose Selflessness

*By Ross Shafer*

## Why Read This Story?

*Savior faire is the French phrase for: "the ability to act or speak appropriately in social situations." We would all love to be able to do that. If you could focus on developing just one character trait you would be proud of, what would it be?*

I worked at a comedy club in the heart of Cambridge, Massachusetts. MIT was on one side of this neighborhood and Harvard was on the other side.

Before my Friday night show, I was invited to a Harvard University communications event for some Q & A about success in life and careers. I found the following question fascinating:

STUDENT: "You've met a lot of interesting people in your career. Of all the character traits you've experienced (honesty, integrity, kindness, humor, resilience, or being driven), what do you think is the most important trait we should get right?"

ROSS: "I've never been asked that question. You Harvard kids are much smarter than advertised! Give me a minute."

My first thought was, does this person really think honesty, kindness, and integrity are optional? My second thought was that resilience and drive might be obvious.

I finally said, "I wouldn't choose any of the personality traits you listed. I would choose humility."

(Puzzled looks)

"So, I guess we need to talk about what humility means in the context of success. What do you think it means?"

The answers were all over the board:

"Humility is the opposite of confidence, right?"

"Being humble sounds like I'm happy to be poor."

"Is humility like giving to a charity?"

"Humility is weakness masquerading as nice."

I could see that my choice of best trait might not have been resonating with the room. So, I looked up a Bible scripture I recalled from Sunday school:

"When pride is present, then comes disgrace, but with humility comes wisdom."

That's what I meant when I said the personality trait of humility reigns supreme.

The most impressive business leaders, entertainers, teachers, and professionals I know have possessed an abundance of humility. They put others ahead of themselves and thus make themselves invaluable (and worthy of adoration) to the rest of us.

I would go so far as to say that humility is the cornerstone of all other personality traits.

If you are humble, arrogance doesn't get in the way of your honesty.

If you are humble, pride doesn't hinder you from thinking you are above basic kindnesses.

If you are humble, you don't dismiss the consequences your drive has on others.

If you are humble, your sense of humor is likely to be self-deprecating—the skill of poking fun at yourself instead of others.

How did we get so far away from understanding the meaning of humility?

I blame the folks at Merriam-Webster.

Humility means "the state of being humble." Duh! Both words have their origin in the Latin word humilis, meaning "low." Humble can be used to describe what is ranked low by others, as in "persons of humble origins." People also use the word to describe themselves and things associated with themselves. If you refer to your home as your "humble abode," you are saying that neither you nor your home is very impressive.

I've met a lot of movie stars, politicians, and corporate CEO's. The best of them don't see humility as a "low rank." If they rose from "humble beginnings" they honored those days and usually thought of being humble as a "character builder."

As you've already read in this book, my television host idol was Johnny Carson. Talk about humble beginnings. He grew up in Avoca, Iowa, and Norfolk, Nebraska. When I hosted *The Fox Late Show* I competed directly against Johnny. After I got the job, Johnny sent me a warm handwritten note congratulating me and wishing me luck during the writers' strike. A month or so later, I saw Carson in person at Granita (a Wolfgang Puck restaurant in Malibu). I caught his eye, walked over, and asked him, "What advice would you give a fledgling talk show host?" Johnny said, "Never try to be the best guest on your own show." That's a master's course in humility! Make the guest look good and you'll have a successful show.

I only spent 60 minutes with the former CEO of General Electric, Jack Welch, as we were about to sit on a business panel for Motorola. "Neutron Jack" was a bigger than life, outspoken leader who overflowed with sharp insights. However, you would never mistake his bluster for arrogance.

If you met Jack—even for five minutes—he would ask you a flurry of questions about you. He wanted to know what got you fired up, or what made you sad. He would use your name when he talked to you. Then, a week or so later, you would get a handwritten note from Jack telling you how happy he was to meet you—and how he wished he could have spent more time with you. (I have two such humble notes.) Do you do that?

I've met three U.S. Presidents, but my favorite was George H.W. Bush. If anybody has a right to kick humility to the curb it's a decorated war hero, former director of the CIA, Vice President to Ronald Reagan, and the 41st President of the United States.

I had the honor of co-headlining a talk with him in Dallas, on the subject of innovation. Afterward, I did a 30-minute interview with him in front of 4,000 stockbrokers.

Before the show, I waited in the "green room" until a Secret Service agent (obvious spiral earpiece) came in, "Who are you?" I told him my name and said, "Where should I be?"

"Not here. Down the hall. First room on the right." (I assumed the hall had to be cleared for the President's entrance.)

I left, found the room, walked in, and there was George H.W. Bush...eating a hot dog!

It was just the two of us.

He turned and said, "Ross, right? (sticks out his hand) George Bush."

What!??!! HE's introducing himself to me!? Then he says, "Hey sorry, this is the last hot dog. If you want one, I'm sure that guy will fetch it. So, what's your deal? I mean what're you gonna cover?"

We compare notes and talk for 15-20 minutes. Nicest, most engaging, most humble world leader...EVER! He wanted to talk about comedy. "Hey, do you know any of the comedians my age?" I told him that one of my best friends was comedian Mort Sahl. He lit up and said, "Oh God, I love Mort. Tell him to call me." (Mort has 41's phone number?)

When our time was over, President Bush got whisked away by the Secret Service.

Ok, I was blown away. I just talked to a former President like a new pal.

But what impressed me most was that he made a point to come back to that room to shake my hand and say, "That was fun. I hope I run into you down the trail." And somewhere in my brain I reflexively knew to say, "I do too, sir."

Probably won't surprise you that I finally got those Harvard students to understand the meaning of humility.

## What's In This For You?

*Humility is the highest honor you can bestow on others.*
*When you exercise humility, every other personality*

*trait will take care of itself. Don't allow your "station in life" to fool you into being a know-it-all ass. Remain curious and interested in other people. Life will be much easier on you.*

# CHAPTER 30

# Change Fearlessly

*By Allison Dalvit*

## Why Read This Story?

*If you are feeling bored by your career, or unfulfilled with your life choices, then maybe your mental or emotional confidence has been derailed. This story will help you get it back.*

Full disclosure: I'm not the kind of person who reads motivational books or listens to positive attitude books on tape. I take life at face value and have never seen the value in paper cheerleading.

That is until I met Ross Shafer. His website tagline said, "America's Funniest Motivator." I didn't even know that was a profession. All I knew was that we could talk for hours and he held my attention. The more we dated, the more I fell for his easy-going personality.

During one of our 'good morning' chats, I asked him, "What keeps you busy when you're not traveling to speak to corporate groups?" He told me he was noodling ideas for his next book.

Ross had already written nine books and fourteen human resource training films. Along the way, he had influenced tens of thousands of smart people to unlock what had previously been their paralyzed potential. In one of his three careers, Ross created a comedy TV show (*Almost Live!*) that was on the air for 30+ years. That platform gave rise to such stars as Bill Nye the Science Guy, sitcom lead Joel McHale (*Community*), and Oscar-nominated screenwriter Bob Nelson (*Nebraska*).

Now, he was sketching out a book he had stewing in him for years. He had written enough business tomes and wanted to write a blunt advice book so his offspring could avoid the pitfalls that had devoured so much of his life. Ross laughed, "I have two sons, a daughter, and four grandchildren so the market for this book is admittedly small." What pitfalls was he talking about?

Ross explained he had been poor and then rich, then poor, and finally rich again. He had been madly in love and then unceremoniously dumped. He had been a workaholic and then unemployed. Married and divorced often. He had been obscure and then internationally famous.

The common denominator in his life was his spirit of relentlessness. After surviving all of the above, he was finally hoping to share his favorite tips, tricks, and unconventional words of wisdom for coming out on top. This book was to be bold, gutsy—a warts-and-all useful guidebook for future Shafer generations. He wanted to call it "Two Words of (In Your Face) Advice." Each story in the book would start with two catchy words, accompanied by an essential life lesson.

I loved the idea of this book.

For fun, I started brainstorming word pairs that might become titles for his stories. My morning routine was to sit by my fireplace with a cup of coffee and organize two disparate words that might trigger inspiring life lessons. When I had a good list, I'd text them to Ross (along with a good morning love note). He was tickled by my "work" and each pair of words would ignite some lively chat.

Ross loved my enthusiasm so much that he pitched that I take a stab at writing some of my own stories for his book.

Ross is a sneaky man—he got the woman who doesn't buy into external motivation to transmute random words into an exploration of my potential as a writer.

Me…a writer? Naw. You see, I'm a television producer, not an author. But hey! We were in the middle of a pandemic with nothing but free time. So, I started writing. I was surprised the stories were pouring out of me. It was therapeutic. I should have done this years ago. I would wake up at 3 a.m. with an idea and race to my laptop. I had to peck out the words so I wouldn't forget. I'd be driving and make voice notes on my phone. Me! I didn't even know my phone took audio notes.

I was blown away by the process. I truly didn't know this was in me. Ross kept encouraging me to write whatever came into my head. "Don't edit yourself, just spew!" he said. He made me feel like Michelangelo sculpting David, powerful and inspired. Creating something out of nothing.

I began to realize why Ross was a successful motivator. Between Ross and gallons of coffee, I started thinking I could do this.

Ross taught me how to add emotion and context to shape my stories. I developed a new confidence in my ability to try things.

Then, he hired my daughter Cass, who had just graduated

from the University of Colorado. Cass has an English degree and we gave her a chance to exercise those muscles to punch up my stories.

It might sound suspicious for an experienced writer like Ross to recruit two amateurs (i.e., unpaid). You might think he was just using us behind the scenes, and that he'd end up taking all the credit.

You would be wrong.

He sees his mission in life to prod the rest of us to push beyond our usual safe zones. If you play along, you end up motivating yourself. Ross knows that real results give rise to fresh ideas; which awaken confidence.

I told you he was sneaky.

The most writing I'd done, to date, was a 1,500-word essay in college. In just a few weeks, I'd put down 18,000 words toward a book I never intended to write.

A month passed and I had scribed a total of 40,000 words. I'd caught the fever of Ross's vision.

This was an opportunity to teach.

Life doesn't come with an infallible instruction manual. We simply did our best to share our top survival tips. For Ross and me, the rewards will come in the form of helping you avoid the mistakes that stole too much of our time, too much of our money, and too many years of unnecessary heartache.

By the way, our children will still get this book for Christmas. They will know exactly how we got here, and maybe how to weather storms they cannot possibly see on the horizon.

## What's In This For You?

*Maybe you don't have a professional encourager in your life. But you can do that job yourself by trying some new things you thought were impossible. Writing. Snowboarding. A new language. A musical instrument. Yoga. Chess. Stock trading. Change up your normal routines. Don't listen to anyone who says, "You are too old to do something like <u>that</u>. Besides, you don't know anything about <u>that</u>." Nobody can possibly know your capacity for growth, except you. Try it, secretly if you have to, and then judge how the results make you feel.*

## What's Your Story of Tragedy-To-Triumph?

We hope this book will inspire you to remember
your own life experiences of achieving success...
then failure...and what you did to find success again.

If you would like us to share YOUR STORY
in our future books, please go to:

https://rossshafer.com/topics/
rattled-how-to-go-from-shook-to-solid/

# Photograph Credits

Photographs were provided courtesy
of the authors except for the following:

Page 22: © National Geographic Television

Page 29: © Crystal Gayle © Harrah's Hotel-Casino

Page 30: © John Ascuaga's Nugget Hotel

Page 43: © ABC Television © Fox Broadcasting Network
© KING-TV Seattle

Page 57: © KING-TV Seattle

Page 79: © University of Puget Sound © Marty Nakayama

Page 85: © Painting by Juan Medina

Page 92: © Jeff Abraham

Page 93: © nice.com

Page 132: © Tacoma News Tribune

Page 133: © Just For Laughs Magazine

Page 148: © Budd Friedman © A & E's Evening at The Improv
© National Speakers Association